Creative Destruction and the Sharing Economy

NEW THINKING IN POLITICAL ECONOMY

Series Editor: Peter J. Boettke, *George Mason University, USA*

New Thinking in Political Economy aims to encourage scholarship in the intersection of the disciplines of politics, philosophy and economics. It has the ambitious purpose of reinvigorating political economy as a progressive force for understanding social and economic change.

The series is an important forum for the publication of new work analysing the social world from a multidisciplinary perspective. With increased specialization (and professionalization) within universities, interdisciplinary work has become increasingly uncommon. Indeed, during the 20th century, the process of disciplinary specialization reduced the intersection between economics, philosophy and politics and impoverished our understanding of society. Modern economics in particular has become increasingly mathematical and largely ignores the role of institutions and the contribution of moral philosophy and politics.

New Thinking in Political Economy will stimulate new work that combines technical knowledge provided by the 'dismal science' and the wisdom gleaned from the serious study of the 'worldly philosophy'. The series will reinvigorate our understanding of the social world by encouraging a multidisciplinary approach to the challenges confronting society in the new century.

Titles in the series include:

Creative Destruction and the Sharing Economy

Uber as Disruptive Innovation

Henrique Schneider

Chief Economist, Swiss Federation of SME, Switzerland

NEW THINKING IN POLITICAL ECONOMY

Edward Elgar
PUBLISHING

Cheltenham, UK • Northampton, MA, USA

Published by
Edward Elgar Publishing Limited
The Lypiatts
15 Lansdown Road
Cheltenham
Glos GL50 2JA
UK

Edward Elgar Publishing, Inc.
William Pratt House
9 Dewey Court
Northampton
Massachusetts 01060
USA

A catalogue record for this book
is available from the British Library

Library of Congress Control Number: 2016949984

This book is available electronically in the **Elgar**online
Economics subject collection
DOI 10.4337/9781786433435

ISBN 978 1 78643 342 8 (cased)
ISBN 978 1 78643 343 5 (eBook)

Typeset by Columns Design XML Ltd, Reading

Printed on FSC-certified paper

Printed and bound in Great Britain by Marston Book Services Ltd, Oxfordshire

Contents

Preface

This is a book on Uber. But it is about more than that. It is about an important question in economics: What is the relation between creative destruction and regulation? Uber is a good case for studying this relation. After all, it has been hailed an – or even *the* – example for creative destruction. And it is at stake with regulation in a large number of cases in the United States, Europe, Asia and Latin America. If Uber is an agent of creative destruction, how is it being impacted by regulation? The inverse question can also be asked. How does Uber impact regulation? And how does this all relate to the sharing economy?

So many questions – what are the answers?

Economists and other social scientists are generally interested in abstract lessons to learn. They want to know if there is any general pattern in the relation of Uber, its creative destruction and the way in which it is impacted by regulation or it impacts regulation. Then they want to know if this pattern can be generally applied to other and similar cases – for example, to the sharing economy at large. Economists and social scientists usually look for what they refer to as 'generalizable knowledge.'

This book combines both: the interest in Uber as a unique business model and the more general preoccupation for abstract patterns. This approach has two main advantages. On the one hand, it makes it easier to think about the economic relation between creative destruction and regulation by reviewing a well-known and timely case. On the other hand, this approach helps to understand Uber as such. Many things that Uber is claimed to be – for example, an innovator, a disruptive agent or a game-changer – become clearer once they have been explained within their economic rationale. Besides, there are a lot of economic expressions used around Uber that sound straightforward … but are not. Examples are creative destruction, sharing economy or competition regulation. This books make them clearer – or debunks them.

What can economics learn from Uber? And how does economics help to understand the Uber-effect on other businesses? These two questions are important. They warrant answers. And that is what this book sets out to do.

On a normative note, this book does not intend to justify Uber's actions or to defend the company against the criticisms it faces. The author of this book does not have any affiliation or connection to Uber, its investors or people employed by the company – indeed, the author has never used any service provided by Uber. The reason for it is not ideological; this author just considers Uber to be too complicated – for him – to use. Hailing a cab still has some charm ...

The author of this book would like to thank the following colleagues: Mark Sagoff, who pressed for the book to be written; Eirik Harris Lang, who was sympathetically skeptical about this project but was the main idea-giver; Felix Engelhard, who is a taxicab-industry expert and competitor of Uber – however, with sympathies toward that company. The Free Market Road Shows 2015 and 2016 served as platforms for testing and discussing many of the arguments used in the book. Declan James Ganley and John Chisholm inspired much of the entrepreneurial thinking. The Spring 2016 class in Managerial Economics (Lucerne) had to cope with their teacher's increased interest for Uber, which often translated into more homework. The editors and crew at Edward Elgar Publishing have done their best to make the book readable and marketable; special thanks go to the series editor, Peter Boettke, to the commissioning editor, Alan Sturmer, and the anonymous reviewers.

Introduction

Uber – an app that links private taxi drivers with customers – has encountered several roadblocks around the world: a Brussels court banned it, a Berlin court ruled that the taxis are rental cars and must therefore return to their place of business between each fair, Paris briefly instituted a rule that an Uber cab had to wait for 15 minutes before picking up a passenger regardless of how far apart the two initially were, and the company has run into similar bumps in the road in several American cities.

At the same time, New York City, Paris and Berlin, are all restricting the use of Airbnb, an app analogous to Uber, but for short-term rental of private apartments. In New Jersey the sale of Tesla electric cars might soon come to a halt because of an obscure ruling mandating that cars should be sold through independent car dealers and not directly from producer to consumer as Teslas are.

Why such zeal from local city halls and court rooms in regulating the conduct of business? It seems that this is just the latest installment of the age-old wheel of 'creative destruction': whenever a new product or service is invented – whatever may be its benefits – there will be both winners and losers. One could argue that it is the job of politicians everywhere to balance the costs and benefits of new innovations and block those that do not benefit society as a whole. And that the consequences for those who have long been employed as taxi drivers, in the case of Uber, should be given extra weight.

It seems that in practice, however, the interests of the incumbent taxi companies, hotel owners and car dealerships have much greater weight than the potential gain to local consumers and new companies. As Mr. Leipold, the chairman of Berlin's taxi association, put it, 'This isn't a student start-up against a big taxi cartel. Uber is backed by Google. If I'm wearing gym shorts, I don't want to compete against someone wearing hobnailed boots.'

If incumbents indeed believe they have the right to only compete against student start-ups it seems we might have too little and not too much 'creative destruction.' (Morten Olsen 2014)[1]

Creative destruction, disruptive innovation, potentially revolutionary business models and regulation stopping them: that is what Olsen's blog is about. And it is also what this book is about.

Creative destruction is a force in economic development first described by the Austrian-American economist Joseph Schumpeter (1883–1940) and developed in detail by the American economist and business scholar

Clayton M. Christensen (born 1952). Since the emergence of the digital economy, creative destruction is a widely used term. However, creative destruction and regulation more often than not are at odds with each other. Some economists would push this claim even further. They would say that creative destruction and regulation are by necessity natural opposites. The reason is that while creative destruction is about innovation, or the advancement of new ideas turning them into new products, or business models, thus challenging the status quo of the markets, regulation is about perpetuating this status quo. In the case of Uber, the creative destruction it is supposed to unleash is being stopped by regulation that prefers traditional taxicab providers.

Granted, regulation often envisages maintaining or enhancing the wellbeing or at least the welfare of a society. However, very often regulation fails to achieve this aim and even more often it falls prey to special interests. These, again, are mostly about preserving the status quo. Also here some economists would push the claim further than this. They would say that even if regulation maintains the wellbeing of a society by continuing the present state of affairs, this continuation is detrimental to possible future gains in welfare and wellbeing. When regulation in the short-sighted interest of the present prevents creative destruction from happening, it does so at the expense of future developments. In sum, by privileging the present over the future, regulation opposes innovation.

Uber illustrates this intuition very well. Most of those protesting Uber worldwide do not demand any new regulation. They just call for the existing regulation to be applied to Uber. As local regulators decide about that, they either make Uber comply with existing regulation or they outlaw Uber simply because it is not a taxicab company as regulators know them. No regulator explicitly sets out to curb innovation in the taxi business, but because of the static and backward-looking character of regulation, regulators tend to block the innovator.

Naturally, regulation and regulators don't explicitly claim that opposition to innovation is the goal of their actions,[2] so it becomes difficult to make a case for them actively undermining it. But there is implicit opposition, as the example of Uber shows. This means there are side effects of regulatory activity that are detrimental to innovation. The question, then, is if these side effects can be avoided. If they are a natural part of any regulation, they cannot. From the economic point of view taken here, there are two good reasons, maybe even three, for believing that these side effects are implicit components of – possible all – regulatory activities. They have been hinted at above.

First, regulation is static in nature and prefers the static over the dynamic. This is not a normative claim and it is not meant pejoratively. To state that regulation prefers the static amounts to saying that it is geared toward judging state of affairs and not processes of innovation. By definition, regulation remains unchanged in order to ensure legal certainty and stability. Also by definition, regulation and regulators, when judging facts, interpret them as a function of the static regulation to which they are committed. Call this their frame of reference. This leads to them transforming dynamic developments into static snapshots and interpreting these in the light of static rules. Innovation, as the result of a series of dynamic processes, escapes this mechanism. There is no guarantee – not even plausibility – that a given snapshot can be representative of the whole innovative dynamic. Regulation, therefore, is not suited to deal with innovation because of its static point of view. Apply this to the example of Uber: without taking into consideration what gains consumers and the taxicab industry itself could have from Uber's innovation, regulators decided to look at a snapshot. This shows Uber as an unregulated taxi business competing against regulated service providers. The main point of Uber, however, is missing in this picture: innovation on the level of process, technology, sourcing and quality.

Second, regulation is backward looking. Again, this is not a normative claim and it is not meant pejoratively. To state that regulation is backward looking amounts to saying that past knowledge is its own frame of reference. It has been set up in the past and reflects, therefore, past knowledge and past regulatory intent. Because of the manner regulation is made it cannot incorporate future developments, including innovation. Even if regulation is changed, it is still changed in a backward-looking way, since adapting it to actuality does not mean adapting it to the future – for the future is unknown. Regulators don't know what tomorrow will bring. Regulations and regulators in judging or regulating innovation by current standards, models and methods automatically give preference to what they already know. And that is the status quo. Granted, no one knows how the future is going to unfold. But the difference between regulators and all other participants of a society is while average participants don't take it upon themselves to decide how a society will or should develop, regulators are often in the position of making decisions about it, or at least their decisions have consequences for the future. While regulators have the power to influence the future, it is debatable if they really can know more about it than the average members of a society. Apply this to the example of Uber: regulators compared the novelty – Uber – to what they were accustomed to – traditional taxicabs. Using their current, backward-looking knowledge about taxicabs, the regulators barred Uber *because* it was not a traditional taxicab company. Or they made Uber convert to one in order to make it fit into their backward-looking frame of reference. In doing this, they are imposing the past on the future.

There might even be a third reason for regulation being implicitly opposed to innovation. That is the role of vested interests. Regulation often protects those companies that are already active in a given market over newcomers. This can happen explicitly, when regulation is developed in dialogue with the regulated entities, or implicitly, when the regulated firms constitute the frame of reference for setting up regulation. It is easier to develop regulation by calling the active taxicab companies to a roundtable and discussing with them rather than to do it on the drawing board. And even if the drawing board approach is taken, most regulators first survey the actual status of the industry they want to regulate. Both these methods lead to a preference for insiders over outsiders. Apply this to the example of Uber: in most cities and regions where Uber has been banned, there are institutionalized dialogues between regulators and taxi companies. Uber, however, does not sit at that roundtable.

This third reason for the opposition of innovation and regulation leads to an interesting problem in the dynamic view: What is the role played by participants in markets (or, as economists like calling them, agents)? Often, market agents begin as innovators and drivers of creative destruction, but once they gain a standing in the markets, they develop an interest for protecting their achievements. More often than not, these agents seek regulation as protection in order to solidify their position and prevent even newer innovators from challenging their products. It is not uncommon for those seeking regulation to advance arguments like consumer protection, job security or, as the blog at the beginning of this introduction states, the narrative of David fighting Goliath[3] in order to give their special interests a broader and more social foundation.

What does this tell us? Market agents are not passive bodies pushed by the forces of creative destruction and regulation; they are a force in themselves tending toward the one or the other, as it best suits their interests. It may even be that a given agent has a commitment toward innovation in its mission statement and vision; however, this does not prevent this agent from changing the role it plays. Even a company committed to innovation can start lobbying regulators for more regulation, especially to bar newcomers from joining the market and destroying its established business model. So, it is not about what individual agents claim to prefer, it is about what they actually do, or the role they actually play.[4] As the philosopher Henry Rosemont (2015) put it: 'Role is self.'

Does this mean that all those companies – Uber, Airbnb, Tesla – portrayed by Olsen in his blog as suffering setbacks today because of regulation might embrace it tomorrow? Potentially, not: probably, yes. Does it also mean that some consumers who now hail the advent of those business models might one day change their minds? Possibly, yes. And why is that so? Because markets, more precisely all agents in markets, are in constant change about what they want and what they perceive desirable. Markets are a series of dynamic processes. For this reason, it is not possible to write about Uber, or about the sharing economy, without taking a closer look at the market processes that are behind them. This book is asking questions about Uber, the sharing economy, creative destruction or if regulation is sorting out different processes that occur at the same time but with different directions.

WHAT IS THIS BOOK ABOUT?

This is a book about Uber. More precisely it is about Uber as a case study for the economics of the relation between creative destruction and regulation. So, this book is about innovation – treated here under the concepts of creative destruction and disruptive innovation – regulation – with a focus on sectorial regulation and competition regulation – and, yes, Uber, and more generally the sharing economy.

The book narrates the following story: while creative destruction and disruptive innovation change the entrepreneurial landscape, regulation, especially regulation of sectorial markets and competition regulation, delays this change or even brings it to a halt. Uber, as a participant of the market, is not just an object moved by these two opposing forces. It plays an active role, first as an agent of creative destruction and then possibly in championing regulation on its own terms.

In order to narrate this story, the book touches on a number of questions within economics and its relationship to regulation. Grounded in a particular understanding of the economic concept of the market as a series of processes (see the detailed discussion in Chapter 1), the book relies on economic theory in order to discover the implications of creative destruction, competition regulation and the role that businesses, or market agents, play. It is committed to interdisciplinary thinking, so it also relies on philosophy, jurisprudence, sociology and even history. Instead of discussing these relations in a purely abstract manner, the book uses Uber as a case study. Uber makes these abstract problems tangible and helps, maybe, in recognizing general patterns.

The relationship between Uber, regulation and innovation is by far not the only issue that can be raised by what is often referred to as the Uber phenomenon at least using Uber as a case study. Some examples for these other questions are: Uber's behavior as an economic agent has consequences on people and other companies as well as on the economy and society as a whole. Also, Uber has been treated as a token for the sharing economy, an economic model in which individuals are able to borrow or rent assets owned by someone else. And even more generally, Uber and the sharing economy are often hailed as the ultimate game-changers in capitalism. These are very broad questions about social philosophy, business ethics and the nature of our economic exchanges – assuming there is anything like this. Although these questions are not at the center of this book, they must be addressed: Chapter 1 will examine the question about the often-claimed revolutionary nature of the sharing economy. Chapter 2 discusses Uber's business model and will at least point toward some of the social and ethical implications it might have.

The book focuses on Uber as a case study for analysing and explaining two opposite forces: innovation and regulation. These forces are antagonistic because regulation often delays or stops innovation. Innovation itself can be understood in different ways: there can be technological innovation or just innovative marketing of products; there is innovation in industrial production as well as innovation in organization, among others. The case of Uber shows that a company can pursue different types of innovation at the same time. *Maybe the case of Uber shows that the more diversified a company innovates, the stronger agent of creative destruction it becomes.*

But regulation has different facets. Regulation can be broadly understood as the entirety of a legal system. It can also be thought of as sectorial regulation envisaging setting standards, for example, for the quality of services provided or the security of customers. Regulation can also be about some types of market processes, for example, about competition. The case of Uber shows that regulation can be an amalgamation of all three. However, sectorial regulation and competition regulation impact Uber the most. So this book will focus on these two aspects. *Maybe the case of Uber shows that the finer-grained the regulation, the more adverse effects on innovation it creates.*

Finally, there is the role that companies play between innovation and regulation. Even Uber seems to be adapting to regulation. This leads Uber to change its business model and value propositions. *Maybe the case of Uber shows that the more innovators adapt to regulation, the more vulnerable they become to creative destruction by even newer agents with even more disruptive innovation.*

THE WAY FORWARD

The book consists of four chapters. Each is dedicated to a leading question. All chapters share the same basic structure. First, the question is outlined, then it is discussed using the framework of economic theory. Finally, the results of the discussion are applied to Uber. Each chapter ends with a summary that is the answer to the leading question. The four chapters and their leading questions are:

- What is the economics of Uber (and this book)? It has been mentioned above that this book understands markets as processes; as an open-ended multi-polar series of exchanges. This understanding requires a more detailed explanation. This explanation also helps in understanding how this conception of the market as processes differs from the conception of markets that most regulators share, which is considering them an institution. This explanation sets the theoretical ground for investigating the relation between innovation and regulation. Then, the chapter provides an overview on the special setting of Uber as an economic phenomenon. This setting is often referred to as the sharing economy. The first chapter of the book discusses what might be new about the sharing economy and how it might be different from other, usual markets.
- What is Uber's business model? The second chapter of the book is Uber-specific. Without going into too much detail, the most important aspects of Uber as a company, its strategy and business model are explored. Its technology, unique features, diversification of product lines and market penetration tactics are at the center of this chapter. After all, it is about showing on what levels Uber innovates. Also, this chapter contains a brief history of the taxicab industry and its regulation, which helps highlight the specific differences of Uber. This brief history also helps in understanding why taxicab regulation is as it is today.
- How is Uber an agent of creative destruction? In the third chapter, two distinct but complementary ideas of innovation are discussed: Schumpeter's creative destruction and Christensen's disruptive innovation. So much has been written about them that it is the aim of this chapter to go back to the roots, back to the original texts. While Schumpeter came up with the idea of creative destruction, it was Christensen that made it operational. After explaining both theories, the chapter applies them to the case of Uber.

- How opposite are innovation and regulation? The fourth chapter provides a more detailed survey of the relation between innovation and regulation. It asks which arguments for regulation can be put forward and how their respective economics work. In particular, it looks at how the economics of so-called pro-competitive regulation impacts innovation. Special attention is given to sectorial regulations and the regulation of competition. After this discussion, the idea of regulation and innovation opposing each other is applied to Uber's case. How Uber changes its business model because of regulation – in order to accommodate it – is explored. But, on the other hand, it is also shown that some regulations are starting to change in order to accommodate Uber.

After these four chapters, a conclusion asks the last question: Who is or will be destroying Uber, the disruptor? Here the focus is on the role of market agents, especially about how Uber changed its role and how it might start to play the regulatory game. If it starts, then other agents will try to innovatively disrupt Uber.

With this approach, each chapter can be read on its own or used in a classroom situation. Also, with this approach, the reader advances through different parts of economic theory and different stages of Uber's development (so far). Continuously mirroring economic theory on Uber reveals the double intent of this book: it is a book on Uber and it is a book on economics.

NOTES

1. While the relevant academic references are quoted in the reference section, news and blogs are referred to in these notes. Olsen, M. (2014), 'The fight against creative destruction,' accessed 20 May 2016 at http://blog.iese.edu/economics/2014/04/23/the-fight-against-creative-destruction.
2. But the author of this book attended a podium in France in March 2015 during which a competition regulator said 'Everything that had to be invented, exists already.'
3. In its broad meaning, the story is about an underdog situation, a contest where a smaller, weaker opponent faces a much bigger, stronger adversary, and wins. The biblical story – with a different and religious intention – can be found in 1 Samuel 17.
4. See, for a non-Uber example, the strange case of the Swiss bank Credit Suisse. This bank is openly committed to innovation. On its strategy papers, it claims that 'innovation is a must.' And even in practice, Credit Suisse is an incremental innovator. However, its Chairman of the Board, Urs Rohner, in 2015 openly demanded a worldwide regulation of all banks. It seems strange for a bank to call for more regulation. But the rationale behind it is simple once revealed: due to its large structure – Credit Suisse is one of the largest banks on the planet – it would be cheaper for this bank to implement regulation than for other banks. The scale of its structure diminishes average costs of compliance. Credit Suisse would have a competitive advantage over other banks because of regulation-induced costs. So, here,

Credit Suisse plays the role of a market agent preferring regulation over its own commitment to innovation. The irony is that Credit Suisse could compete with other agents on quality, price or innovation, but prefers to compete using regulation-induced costs. For Credit Suisse's commitment to innovation, see Credit Suisse (2016), 'Innovation in the service of clients,' accessed 20 May 2016 at https://www.credit-suisse.com/cl/en/about-us/who-we-are/history/innovation.html. For Rohner's comments, see the podium at the World Economic Forum 2015 in Davos, for example, in https://www.youtube.com/watch?v=4ZkvsuRp4dM (marks 16:07 and 55:20; accessed 20 May 2016).

1. What is the economics of Uber (and of this book)?

What is so special about Uber? Consumers are used to dealing with different companies and brands. They buy vegetables and meat, home appliances and apparel, cars and tools, go to the hairdresser and to a restaurant, take counsel from a lawyer or from an accountant. These are all companies; some of them are even branded. The customer, however, only seldom identifies her person with the company she does business with. Even to brands, devotion is very seldom. Uber, however, seems to be more than just a brand – and being a brand is already something special. Uber seems to have not just customers but a 'fellowship': people identify important actions in their lives with the mobility provided by Uber. For the members of this 'fellowship,' Uber gives special meaning to important actions or parts of their lives. For some, Uber is even a worldview, a *weltanschauung*.[1] And if that is already a phenomenon from the sociologist's point of view, from the economist's it is even more overwhelming: Why do people identify themselves with a company to which there are many substitutes? Why do people identify themselves with a company that openly admits monitoring them and surging its prices, whenever its own 'fellowship' gets too attached? Shouldn't this behavior make Uber more exchangeable and not less? Reality shows the opposite to be true.

In addition, Uber is often considered either a phenomenon of its own or a token of the so-called sharing economy. Hailed by some, vilified by others, Uber and the sharing economy established themselves in the lives of many people and in the economies of most countries. And this raises the attention of economists. Can economics describe and analyse Uber or the sharing economy using its current toolbox? Are such fundamental concepts as market, welfare, equilibrium, profit or cost even applicable to the sharing economy? Or are Uber and the sharing economy completely different types of economic endeavor that require a different and new set of theories to be dealt with. Do Uber and the sharing economy revolutionize economics as a science and as a practice?

Uber and the sharing economy pose many important questions even before the start of the case study of this book, which is Uber and the relationship between innovation and regulation. And so, here lies an additional problem: in discussing the implication of Uber and the sharing economy on economics, economic concepts are needed in the first place. Examining if and how fundamentally different both are supposed to be from economics depends on the conception of economics being employed. And this is the task of this chapter: to lay out the book's conception of economics and to describe the sharing economy and Uber within it. In addition, the chapter will reference some conceptions that are dismissed in the theoretic approach chosen in this book and how they might lead to a different analysis of Uber and the sharing economy.

In the first section, the chapter develops a framework for analysing the sharing economy and Uber. In the second section, this framework is applied to the sharing economy. In the third, Uber will be the focus; it is this third section that builds a bridge to the next chapter. A short summary answers the chapter's leading question.

1.1 THE ECONOMIC FRAMEWORK

The economics of this book relies on two fundamental ideas. The first is that individuals are free to act, which means that they are free to choose between alternative actions but are at the same time responsible for their choices. The second is that the notion of a market is best understood as an open-ended, multi-polar, non-determined series of processes. This conception of economics is typical of the Austrian School in Economics. The meaning of 'Austrian School' as well as the two fundamental ideas that are their base are explained in this section.

1.1.1 Austrian School in Economics

The Austrian School in Economics is a heterodox approach to economics. Heterodox means that it is not the mainstream or the majoritarian theory to which most economists subscribe. The Austrian School in Economics is not the only heterodox approach in today's economics. Other are, for example, socialist, Marxian, institutional, evolutionary, land-based (Georgist) or post-Keynesian economics. If these are the heterodox approaches, what is the 'orthodoxy' from which they all deviate? It is the 'neoclassic-Keynesian synthesis.' Blanchard (2008, p. 831) describes the synthesis:

> The term 'neoclassical synthesis' appears to have been coined by Paul
> Samuelson to denote the consensus view of macroeconomics which emerged

in the mid-1950s in the United States. This synthesis remained the dominant paradigm for another 20 years, in which most of the important contributions, by Hicks, Modigliani, Solow, Tobin and others, fit quite naturally. The synthesis had, however, suffered from the start from schizophrenia in its relation to microeconomics [the synthesis uses Keynesian macroeconomics and neoclassical microeconomics, which generated paradoxes], which eventually led to a serious crisis from which it is only now re-emerging.

Mainstream economics is primarily concerned with the results of markets. It subscribes to the idea that markets, macro and micro, tend toward equilibrium. This means that there is an ideal configuration of price and quantity that clears the market. When this configuration is achieved, the interests of all market agents are optimally fulfilled. This is the case, for example, in full employment, optimal economic growth or perfect competition. If a given economy is not in any of these states, there is room for improvement. Specifically, policies based on economic instruments can be used – some would claim must be used – to reach the equilibrium. And how do economists and regulators know the equilibrium configuration? Well, mainstream economics determines that at least theoretically, equilibria configurations for markets can be determined or calculated, even beforehand, by using market data and analytic tools.

Austrian economics – among other heterodox approaches – disagrees with most of this. Mostly because Austrian economics remains agnostic about the results of markets and directs its attention to their constituent elements. For most Austrian economists, it is the preconditions of market processes that matter. These are individual decision-making processes, innovation, subjective discovery of utility, cost or exchange possibilities as well as forms of cooperative practices. The Austrian School in Economics neither tries to reconcile Keynesianism with the so-called classic, laissez-faire approach nor can it be thought of as a monolithic bloc. Austrian economics is a heterodox way of thinking about economics that is itself full of heterodoxies. Boettke (2008) identifies the following ten main propositions that are common to so-called Austrian economists:

1. Only individuals choose: economics, then, explains how these choices were made on which grounds and which consequences – intended and non-intended – they had.
2. The study of the market order is fundamentally about exchange behavior and the institutions within which exchanges take place: economics studies the different series of decisions regarding exchanges and how these institutions are formed.
3. The 'facts' of the social sciences are what people believe and think:

economics and all social sciences deal with social constructions (see also Searle 1995).[2]

4. Utility and costs are subjective: economics is the study of the utility and costs of alternatives in light of the individual's subjective point of view.

5. The price system economizes on the information that people need to process in making their decisions: economics sees prices as the results of the different choices and exchanges in which individuals engage; individuals use prices as bearers of information about the choices of other individuals, that is why prices are relative in nature and are relative to the individual economic agent.

6. Private property in the means of production is a necessary condition for rational economic calculation: without private property, the individual is not able to reflect all subjective calculations of utilities and costs of choices into the decision to act.

7. The competitive market is a process of entrepreneurial discovery: competition is an open-ended, non-determined process of discovery of innovation, but also of individual discovery of utilities and costs.

8. Money is non-neutral: as money enters the economy, it influences relative prices; since prices are a function of individual utility and cost calculations, money entering the economy impacts each agent differently on each relation of relative price.

9. The capital structure consists of heterogeneous goods that have multi-specific uses that must be aligned: production is always for an uncertain future demand, and the production process requires different stages of investment; the values of all producer goods at every stage of production derive from the value consumers place on the product being produced.

10. Social institutions often are the result of human action, but not of human design: social institutions emerge by the common or cooperative practices of those social agents engaged in exchange; if these agents grow disinterested in one specific social practice, that practice ceases existing altogether; if agents start a new social practice, a new social institution emerges. Agents following other agents in a social practice is the constitutive moment of that institution; not its design.

Boettke (2008) is also clear in stating the result of these propositions:

> The implications of these ten propositions are rather radical. If they hold true, economic theory would be grounded in verbal logic and empirical work focused on historical narratives. With regard to public policy, severe doubt would be raised about the ability of government

officials to intervene optimally within the economic system, let alone to rationally manage the economy.

This list calls for a comment on three peculiarities of Austrian economics. First, these propositions do not mean that all economists belonging to the Austrian School share the same ideas. The ten propositions mentioned here are just a set common to most. And common means something along the lines of Wittgenstein's family resemblance[3] rather than hard criteria by which every single Austrian economist can be distinguished from a non-Austrian one. Second, very often, Austrian economics is identified with right-wing political ideology. This is wrong. There is no necessary connection between Austrian economics and any partisan politics. While it is true that Austrian economists are generally skeptical of state intervention, there have been different self-identified Austrian economists that accepted it to some degree – Schumpeter being one of them. Also, many policies typically championed by right-wing groups are met with disapproval by the majority of Austrian economists, for example, overarching security policy, international (military) engagement, loose monetary policy (even if it is demanded by private agents in the economy), among others.[4]

The third peculiarity, or even oddity, of Austrian economics is that it cannot be found in Austria anymore. Almost all economists inspired by or self-identified with Austrian economics are today in the United States and Canada, as well as some in small pockets in France, Germany, Switzerland, Liechtenstein and Spain. Austrian economics is called such because it began in the University of Vienna. So, when a given economist is called Austrian, it seldom means that the economist is from Austria. Likewise, the adjective Austrian in this book denotes an economist of this persuasion rather than Austrian nationals. Schumpeter is one exception: he was an Austrian national and an Austrian economist. The 'founder' of the Austrian School was also an Austrian national (and a tutor to the crown-prince to the Habsburg Empire; and a champion for giving the poor access to the economy), Carl Menger (1840–1921). Menger came up with the important principle of Austrian economics: the economic values of goods and services are subjective in nature. Bluntly put: what is valuable for you may not be valuable for your peer. With an increase in the number of goods, their subjective value for an individual diminishes. This valuable insight lies behind the concept of what is called subjective diminishing marginal utility. Subjective is the operative word for 'Austrianism.'

Some other well-known Austrian-Austrians are Ludwig von Mises (1881–1973) and Friedrich August von Hayek (1899–1982). Non-Austrian (nationals) Austrians (economists) are Murray Rothbard (1962–1995), Israel Kirzner (born 1930) and Lew Rockwell (born 1944). Some Nobel laureates have been inspired by Austrian economics, for example, James Buchanan (1919–2013) and Vernon Smith (born 1927). Also, the other economist and management scholar mentioned in Chapter 3, Clayton Christensen, has been influenced by Austrian economics. So, Austrian economics is not only the theoretical background from which this book is written. It is also the background or the influence that marked those individuals that came up with the theories behind creative destruction and disruptive innovation. Austrian economics, therefore, is also an appropriate way of reading Schumpeter and Christensen because it is close to their own point of view.[5]

This brief overview on the Austrian School serves as a background to the actual understanding of economics in this book. Here, markets are viewed as a series of open-ended, undetermined processes, or series of individual exchanges. While economists of all persuasions could subscribe to this conception of the market to some degree, it matches best with the Austrian approach. What it means to view the market as a series of processes will be discussed in the next subsection. In case of curiosity, more information about the Austrian School can be found in Grassl and Smith (1986), Boettke (1994) or Schulak and Unterköfler (2011).

1.1.2 Markets as Processes

A characteristic feature of the Austrian approach to economic theory is its emphasis on the market as a process, rather than as a configuration of prices, qualities, and quantities that are consistent with each other in that they produce a market equilibrium situation. This feature of Austrian economics is closely bound up with dissatisfaction with the general use made of the concept of perfect competition. It is interesting to note that economists of sharply differing persuasions within the Austrian tradition all display a characteristic disenchantment with the orthodox emphasis on both equilibrium and perfect competition ... From the Austrian perspective, which emphasizes the role of knowledge and expectations, these explanations take too much for granted. What is needed is a theory of the market process that takes explicit notice of the way in which systematic changes in the information and expectations upon which market participants act lead them in the direction of the postulated equilibrium 'solution.' (Israel Kirzner 1976, 3.1.1 and 3.1.8)

Understanding the market as a series of processes entails giving up the idea of a calculable, predetermined equilibrium. It also means that markets cannot be judged by their results because there are no results, just stages of the processes. This position makes economists focus instead on the different series of discoveries that agents go through when they engage in voluntary exchange. In this view, markets are open-ended, undetermined processes for satisfying the individual's subjective needs. Of course, these individual needs can change too. They change as a function of the subjective satisfaction or dissatisfaction individuals might have, but they also change according to the individual's context, learning processes and even moods. In the continuous interactions with other people, individuals not only learn but constantly reveal information about their own preferences and decisions. The market as such is just a linguistic marker denoting a series of multi-agent, multi-layered, multi-lateral learning processes.

Therefore, the descriptive term market is understood here as just an abbreviation for (or even a metaphor denoting) a whole conglomerate of processes, interactions and exchanges between individual entities that engage therein freely and without *ex ante* central coordination. The market is a dynamic place to gather and reveal information; as such, it is a dynamic place to learn. Markets consist of the continuous revelation of individual and collective preferences, means-ends calculations, assessments (of the self and the others) and information stocks by its agents; they are choosing individual entities, like the individual or the voluntary group. The outcomes of markets, prices and quantities are but aggregate information about these individual and subjective revealed preferences. The outcomes of market processes have no other quality than being aggregate bearers of information (Kirzner 1996; Schneider 2014). These outcomes cannot be understood in terms of 'good' or 'bad' or even 'ideal,' since they are only 'good,' 'bad' and 'ideal' from the subjective perspective of each agent. If market processes produce what seems to be a distortion or if the results of markets are difficult for economists to explain, in this approach, economists will go back to the study of the general conditions under which market processes unfold themselves. They will ask, for example, which factors influenced decisions, which information flows were available to the agents, how aligned individual choices and the bearing of their consequences were and so on. In this approach, if market processes seem to be generating problematic outcomes, it is analysed whether there is anything in these general conditions preventing individual agents from gathering information, assessing information, making own and subjective decisions and so on. If nothing distorting these preconditions for market processes is found, then all outcomes are to be accepted. Often, this approach will reveal that state agent interventions distort or at least skew the preconditions for the market processes to unfold.

What would be the alternative view of the market? As mentioned earlier, mainstream economics has a different conception. Often, the market is pictured as an institution, that is, a central area of exchange with rules, agents, oversight and a whole array of very real entities and properties (Ross 2014). This institutional conception of the markets shares many aspects with the Austrian idea: both see individual decision-making as pivotal, both pay close attention to the flows of information and to the learning of market agents, both see the market as a plug-and-play situation. However, the differences between both concepts are also important.

One important difference is the mainstream idea that all markets strive for equilibrium. That does not mean that a market-clearing configuration will automatically be reached, but there is always at least one potential optimal situation for every market and this situation can be reached primarily by the market agents through their interactions, secondarily by regulation. Seeing the market as a closed-case institution automatically means assigning a regulatory entity to that institution. While the Austrian approach sees the rules of an institution or of a process as emerging from the cooperative social practice that leads to that institution or process, the mainstream approach sees markets as an initially designed institution. Designed by whom? By the regulator; mostly by the state (Ross 2014).

This difference deserves more emphasis because it is crucial: the institutional understanding of markets believes that there can be no markets without regulations and regulators – they are constitutive of the market. This does not entail that the regulation must necessarily be one by an entity with power over the agents, like the modern-day nation-state. Market agents themselves can come up with the regulation of their market institution. But many contemporary orthodox economists claim that regulation by the nation-state is more effective and more efficient than the self-regulation of market agents (Ross 2014). Why do Austrians oppose this view? Because this institutional view implies that there are hard-fact results of markets and that regulators can anticipate these results. The second implicit assumption is that regulation makes it easier for the market to achieve its predetermined results (or those results that lead to a maximization of welfare; see further below). Most importantly, the third assumption of this view is that the results of markets can be judged objectively. As mentioned before, Austrian economics sees the market more as a way of communication than as a mechanism for reaching a given social goal. Since the results of the market processes underlie open-ended, undetermined dynamics and these results can only be judged individually, it would be overbearing to claim that the market has a teleological goal and that some agent, the regulator, has some epistemic advantage over others and can ultimately decide between the 'good' and the 'bad.'

There is yet another important difference between the institutional view of the markets and the process approach. This institutional view strongly suggests that these regulations, in order to work, cannot and should not be influenced or legally circumvented by individuals. This is the case because markets are not only a place of exchange but also an instrument to promote social welfare. So, regulators use markets in order to promote social welfare. Skeptically, it could be asked now how all the elements – individual responsibility, free-willed exchange, predetermined outcome and the promotion of social welfare – fit together in this institutional view.

Here it gets tricky: promoting social welfare, according to this institutional view of markets is not completely incompatible with individuals' decisions and learning processes. The idea of equilibria comes in handy now. As mentioned before, if a given market reached its configuration of equilibrium, agents are all optimally served. In most points of equilibria, all of the participants of the market have reached their best possible welfare. So, it is the regulator's job to create the best possible conditions for markets to find their optimum states (Ross 2014). But mainstream economics can go even further in the quest for welfare maximization. 'An allocation of resources is Pareto efficient if it is not possible (through further reallocations) to make one person better off without making someone else worse off' (Reetz 2005, p. 26). This sentence is the definition of Pareto efficiency. And upon this idea many postulates of welfare maximization are grounded. Note that the Pareto maxim is about efficiency and not about desirability and note too that it is about the allocation of resources. Welfare economics turns it into the allocation of outcomes and interprets the maxim like this: 'If it is possible to reallocate outcomes in order to make a person better off without making someone else worse off, this reallocation should be pursued' (Reetz 2005, p. 108). With this reformulated Pareto maxim, not only the goal of regulation is stated but also a task is given to the regulator; it has to intervene in the market until the social optimal outcome allocation is achieved.

Here again the Austrian approach disagrees. As mentioned earlier, this institutional theory of markets has a number of flaws: as profoundly dynamic processes, markets have no pre-set equilibrium point, and even if they had, it would be impossible to know them beforehand, or even as they occur, since equilibria constantly change with the dynamic of the process. A third party, for example, the regulator, cannot know more than the information being exchanged in the markets since market agents are at the same time members of the regulatory body (yes, if someone looks into a market, this person becomes an agent). More plainly put: regulators are subjective individuals like those people participating in the market process; they cannot know more about the future than anyone else. If there is no pre-set, optimal equilibrium, the welfare maximization postulate becomes obsolete, since it is necessarily dependent on equilibrium.[6] Also, the welfare maximization postulate presupposes that there is an objective measure for categorizing the output of markets. But from the market process view, there is not. How desirable the outcome of a market process is depends on the subjective value judgement on each market agent. If one market agent is not happy with the outcomes, this person will engage in other exchanges and try to influence the outcome in light of individual preferences. So, if markets are understood as processes, welfare is the individual's or the voluntary group's concern. Through freely deciding, acting and learning, agents will deal with what they individually consider to be their welfare.

The consequences of subscribing to this process-based conception of the market become apparent now. The most important consequence of understanding the market as a form of spontaneous exchange is that there is no optimum, end-state or result that can be assessed a priori, or even before the exchanges occur. This means that no market agent or regulator is in the position of knowing the outcomes of the process of spontaneous exchange since no one knows how individuals or groups of individuals will behave, react, learn, adjust, strategize, change their preferences, think, cooperate, evaluate or even withdraw among other things. The complexity of the free-willed spontaneous exchange rules out the possibility of *ex ante* knowledge about its outcomes. In taking this view, one has to admit that there is no guarantee for innovation being successful or failing, since it is a series of complex processes with multiple possible and interdependent outcomes that will ultimately establish if, how long and under which circumstances a given innovation succeeds and/or fails. In this view, so-called consumer protection is something best done by the individual consumer acting responsibly. Or the individual consumer can organize other individuals into a group and this group could engage in a series of exchanges with one or different suppliers. While this process understanding of the market allows for agents to have individual expectations or desiderata relating the outcomes of markets, they cannot have actual, factual knowledge about it.

What justifies regarding the market as a series of processes? There are two main arguments. The first is logical consistency. If individuals or groups of individuals decide freely what to do, the outcomes of these decisions and their interdependencies are too complex to be known

beforehand. Before the internet, there was no knowledge of the outcomes
of the internet. Before Uber, there was no knowledge of its outcomes.
Even as it started, there was no knowledge of how it would develop and
which impacts it would have. The second argument is what often is
called Ockham's razor,[7] which can be stated as follows: among competing explanations, the one with the fewest assumptions should be selected
(see Ariew 1976). This principle is about the burden of proof. The
explanation that claims more has to prove more. Therefore, if the
institutional view on markets presupposes an optimum, or equilibrium, it
is that view's task to demonstrate that there is one. And that is a difficult
thing to prove. On the other hand, in claiming that the market is just a
series of exchanges, there is less to prove about it. For example, if
someone claims that the outcomes of market interactions can be known,
the burden of proof dictates that it has to be proven how the outcomes
can be known. Sticking to the simpler understanding of the market as the
spontaneous exchange of individuals and groups of individuals is more
consistent with the razor.

With these explanations given, it becomes easier to understand why
this book follows the Austrian approach and conceptualizes markets as
processes. First, creative destruction and disruptive innovation were
developed by authors that subscribed to the Austrian School at large or
were influenced by it. Therefore, it seems fair to discuss their ideas from
the perspective in which they are founded or by which they were
influenced. Creative destruction and disruptive innovation are not just
metaphorical terms or buzzwords; they are, at least, part of economic
theories.

Second, even proponents of the institutional view of markets don't
deny that regulating markets is a difficult endeavor since no one willingly
wants to bring all innovation to a halt. Even regulation cannot be pursued
maximally, just, in their view, to a configuration in which it trades off
gains from regulation and regulation-induced costs (for example, its
negative impact on innovation). So, even these proponents study the
positive and negative effects of regulation on markets and their agents. In
order to determine the equilibrium point of regulation, regulation has to
try to understand the market it is trying to regulate (Armstrong 1999).
Therefore, also from the institutional point of view, an analysis of the
dynamics in a given market is desirable.

Using the conception of markets as a series of processes in this book
means we don't know what the future of the ideal transportation market
is. Taxicab companies do not know it; Uber does not know it; regulators
do not know it; customers do not know it and especially this author does
not know it. The analysis of Uber's activities, regulation and innovation

occurs then in terms of the open-ended, non-determinate dynamic of markets understood as learning processes (and not in terms of supposed equilibria of markets).

1.1.3 Individual Action

Another aspect of the methodology being employed here is that individual action is at the center of attention. It is the individual or the voluntary group of individuals that make decisions about what they want, how to pursue what they want and how to live with the outcomes of their actions. As discussed above, contrary to most other approaches in economics, the Austrian School is not primarily concerned with market institutions, social welfare, money and such, but with actions, adaptations, responsibility, information (beliefs) by the individual or by a voluntary group of individuals and how factors impact on these agents, distorting their decision-making. As long as the preconditions for engaging in the market process – for example, monetary stability, symmetry of risk and responsibility, freedom of choice – are aligned, individuals or voluntary groups will be able to do what they consider best. As soon as these preconditions are distorted, however, individuals and voluntary groups will engage in a downward spiral of maladjustments to the distortions (Kirzner 1996; Mises 1927, 1933). The reason is that the agents in the markets adapt their decision-making to the very factors distorting them. Their individual and subjective calculation of beliefs, preferences and costs starts to encompass elements of which they might profit or by which they might be disadvantaged without having any possibility of either influencing those elements or taking responsibility for them. Distortions, however, have to be separated from possible states of the market process that might be considered undesirable from a subjective perspective. Distortions of the market processes occur when an agent outside the market dictates terms to the processes or agents of the market. When market agents try to dictate terms to one another, they can through the market processes react to it; they cannot, however, react to the agent that dictates its terms to the markets from outside the process. For example, people have no market influence over telephone regulations. But if a single telephone company tries to dictate terms to the users, they just switch to another. The market process disciplines the actions of its agents, that is why even an agent with strong power over a given point of the market process is held in check by the process. State intervention and the like exert power over the market process without the market process being able to discipline the source of power. This is a distortion.

Individuals act and react in market processes based on their own calculations of utility and costs. Innovation and the whole of entrepreneurship are, therefore, the result of or constitute a series of decisions taken by an individual or a voluntary group of individuals. To the contrary, regulation is seen as rules of behavior dictated to individuals or voluntary groups of individuals. Regulation is not ground in the free-willed decisions of the agents. Often, regulation prevents individuals from becoming innovators or entrepreneurs, since both are not only a combination of technical skills, but constituted by what one might call 'taking advantage of the moment.' The more regulation constrains the actions of individuals, the more difficult it becomes to take this advantage. Kirzner (1976, 3.1.14) establishes the link of individual, entrepreneurship and process:

> Misesian theory of human action conceives of the individual as having his eyes and ears open to opportunities that are 'just around the corner.' He is alert, waiting, continually receptive to something that may turn up. And when the prevailing price does not clear the market, market participants realize they should revise their estimates of prices bid or asked in order to avoid repeated disappointment. This alertness is the entrepreneurial element in human action ... At the same time that it transforms allocative decision making into a realistic view of human action, entrepreneurship converts the theory of market equilibrium into a theory of market process.

Of course, regulation could be accepted if it is incurred voluntarily, since then it is one of those decisions taken by individuals. But by the same standard, individuals should be able to opt out of regulations. In this dynamic view, rules would emerge from human action as a certain type of cooperative practice. And since rules are confronted with the steady pressure of human action, they adapt to the needs of the individuals, becoming processes too. Judging how regulation and the individual interact depends on the responses to the following questions: how much influence do individuals have on the regulation, and what can they do if they don't agree with it?

As for the first: if regulations are the direct fruits of decisions by individuals, as they are, for example, among condo owners or by shareholders in businesses, they are not distortions of the preconditions of markets as explained above. These regulations have been incurred voluntarily by the individual and this individual retains the right of opting out, for example, by selling the flat or the shares. Most importantly, as co-owner, the individual has an important role to play in steering this set of rules. Note that, different from political influence, here the individual has a direct influence in the company's strategy or the condo's policies. The individual acts directly and unconditionally upon his co-propriety.

As for the second: even if there are rules upon which the single individual has no direct influence (that is, what economists call exogenous), if the individual can walk away, there is less of a problem with that set of rules. In this case, the rules themselves are submitted to competition and the individual still has the possibility to freely choose what to do. This might be the case in the labor market (if I am not happy with the rules of my employer, I change my job) or with sports clubs (if I don't like the by-laws of my gym, I look for a new one), for example. Note that the individual here has no direct power over the regulation, since employees don't own their employer and customers don't own their suppliers, but by the voluntary actions of employees and customers, the respective sets of rules are under pressure.

The distortion of the individual's liberty to decide and to act begins there, where regulations are dictated to individuals without giving them a say or the opportunity to decide otherwise. For example, before the market entry of Uber, if I wanted to get a cab in New York City I could not change the cab regulation, say, to choose which type of car I want or how to reduce the asymmetry of information concerning the driver's credentials. I basically had to take the cab that the regulation assigned to be driving. Also, I could not take any other type of cab, just the regulated ones. Similar constraints apply if I want to start a taxicab business. I have to adhere to the regulation upon which I have neither influence – at least not as a small- or medium-sized company – nor the possibility to circumvent (legally, of course). There is a distortion of the individual's liberty to decide and act here, because the individual basically cannot decide on what to do, but to comply with exogenous impositions on her behavior. The downward spiral might be that the person starting a taxicab company, despite the initial plan to offer flexible rates or better service, will only offer the regulated industry standard.

To sum up this subsection, while the Austrian School in Economics is the general background for this book's analysis of Uber, the conception of the market as processes is its most important tool. Markets are open-ended, indeterminate series of exchanges by individuals. So, the individual is the pivotal entity. Innovation is the possible consequence of the individual's or the voluntary group's decisions in entrepreneurship. Innovation, however, is no guarantee for success. Success is at best a subjective value judgement about a temporal outcome of the market process. The so-called innovators will learn from their own success and/or failure and adapt their actions and decisions to what they have learned.

1.2   SHARING ECONOMY AND ITS NOVELTY

Now it is time to apply the frame of reference developed above to two subjects: to the sharing economy and to Uber. First, let the sharing economy be considered. What is it? What is new about it? And is there anything essentially different to the sharing economy?

1.2.1   Sharing, Collaborative or Cooperative?

There are many different ways of defining the sharing economy. For starters, there is no single definition. What some call the sharing economy is called by others the collaborative economy or the cooperative economy. But then again, some claim that these expressions denote different phenomena. Keeping in mind that there is a market for definitions, one should not expect one single, all-embracing definition to establish itself. Also keeping in mind that the market is a learning process, one should expect definitions to change as new business models emerge. Rachel Botsman (2015), one of the best-known analysts of the sharing economy, offers an explanation for the diversity of definitions – an explanation not without irony:

> The 'sharing economy' is a term frequently incorrectly applied to ideas where there is an efficient model of matching supply with demand, but zero sharing and collaboration involved. Platforms such as Washio, Deskbeers, Dashdoor, and WunWun that require the tap of an app to instantly access a clean shirt, massage, or keg of beer are fundamentally different from platforms like BlaBlaCar or RelayRides, which are genuinely built on the sharing of underused assets. Pizza Hut and Amazon one-hour delivery aren't the sharing economy, and these on-demand apps are no different; they are mobile-driven versions of point-to-point delivery. They're thrown under the same umbrella as part of the sea change in consumer behavior that uses the smartphone as a remote control to efficiently access things in the real world. This muddiness in terminology is partly coming from Uber. The experience of using geo-location and frictionless payments to change our ability to get a taxi is creating a transformation in terms of how we expect and want to access everything from getting a parcel shipped on Shyp to a dog walked on Wag, with a tap of a screen. But the Uberfication of everything brings with it confusion about what is true sharing.

Not every digital platform is automatically part of the sharing economy. While in today's manifestation, the sharing economy heavily relies on technology, especially the internet, it is not by necessity so. Inversely, not every business or not-for-profit organization with a web presence is engaging in the sharing economy. Botsman (2015) and Botsman and

Rogers (2010) offer five criteria for delineating what it means for a business to be in the sharing economy:

1. The core business idea involves unlocking the value of unused or underutilized assets ('idling capacity') whether it's for monetary or non-monetary benefits.
2. The company should have a clear values-driven mission and be built on meaningful principles including transparency, humanness and authenticity that inform short- and long-term strategic decisions.
3. The providers on the supply side should be valued, respected and empowered and the companies committed to making the lives of these providers economically and socially better.
4. The customers on the demand side of the platforms should benefit from the ability to get goods and services in more efficient ways that means they pay for access instead of ownership.
5. The business should be built on distributed marketplaces or decentralized networks that create a sense of belonging, collective accountability and mutual benefit through the community they build.

Based on these criteria, Botsman (2015) gives a finer-grained set of definitions of the different aspects of what is commonly referred to as the sharing economy:

> Collaborative Economy: An economic system of decentralized networks and marketplaces that unlocks the value of underused assets by matching needs and haves, in ways that bypass traditional middlemen. Good examples: Etsy, Kickstarter, Vandebron, LendingClub, Quirky, Transferwise, Taskrabbit

> Sharing Economy: An economic system based on sharing underused assets or services, for free or for a fee, directly from individuals. Good examples: Airbnb, Cohealo, BlaBlaCar, JustPark, Skillshare, RelayRides, Landshare

> Collaborative Consumption: The reinvention of traditional market behaviors – renting, lending, swapping, sharing, bartering, gifting – through technology, taking place in ways and on a scale not possible before the internet. Good examples: Zopa, Zipcar, Yerdle, Getable, ThredUp, Freecycle, eBay

> On-Demand Services: Platforms that directly match customer needs with providers to immediately deliver goods and services. Good examples: Instacart, Uber, Washio, Shuttlecook, DeskBeers, WunWun

One might disagree with Botsman's categorization. For example, does Uber not involve sharing the car that incidentally often belongs to the driver? But even if there is no complete agreement with Botsman, these criteria and definitions provide a good perspective into the diversity of economic activities or processes that can be understood by the sharing economy. But what drives them? Researchers usually distinguish three different types of drivers in the sharing economy: economic, technological and societal. Economic drivers are: monetization of excess or idle inventory and capacity; increase in financial flexibility; preference for access over ownership; and influx of venture capitalist funding. Technological drivers are: social networking; mobile and devices platform; and e- or online payment systems. There seems to be less consensus about the societal drivers of the sharing economy. Some researchers tend to use the following, or at least some of them: increasing population density; drive for sustainability; desire for community; and generational altruism (Botsman and Rogers 2010; Chase 2015).

But there are not only drivers to the sharing economy, there are also opposing forces. Chase (2015) identifies the following: government officials oppose sharing that disrupts existing regulations; lack of trust between peer-to-peer buyers and sellers; lack of industry-wide reputation systems and data standards; incumbent players view sharing as a threat to their current business models; and uncertainty about which startups will stand the test of time. Note that the last two forces of opposition seem to assume that incumbent companies cannot engage in the sharing economy and only startups can. This assumption is at least theoretically disputable. Equally debatable is the insinuated necessary link between startups and the sharing economy. But from the overall economic perspective, there is an even more pressing question: is there anything radically new in the sharing economy?

1.2.2   Not So Novel

Judging if the sharing economy is radically new depends on the standard for comparison. Is it new in comparison to regulated, institutional markets? Or are the learning processes of the sharing economy new? Are the results of the sharing economy new? If so, what is the basis for such a comparison? Are these results, as they are known today, being compared to the results of the traditional economy, as they are known today? Or are the drivers of the sharing economy being compared to the drivers of the traditional economy? This last question may prove the best entry point for a comparison.

The drivers mentioned in the last subsection do not seem novel altogether. Monetization of excess capacity and inventory? After all, communities of people have shared the use of assets for thousands of years; for example, roads, ships, planes and restaurants. The person travelling in the plane does not own the plane. It is the airline that decided to acquire capacity and share; that means sell its excess. People eating in a restaurant share the space with other guests and, more importantly, with the owner of the restaurant. And even the business model of hotels began as restaurants decided to rent – share – free rooms. What might have intensified is that the scale and scope of the internet has made it easier for asset owners and those seeking to use those assets to find each other. This, however, is not a revolution of the traditional economy. It is just the enlargement of its agents and processes.

What about the increase in financial flexibility and higher influx of venture capitalist funding? Financial flexibility depends on the subjective preferences of agents. In the development of modern economies, financial flexibility has seen continuous expansions – albeit sometimes curbed by regulation. It is only logical that the more flexible individuals are to use their finances, the more opportunities to invest they will seek. For example, it was the increased financial flexibility and the intention of shared entrepreneurship that made investors create the first limited participation company and call their owners 'shareholders.' The investors share an investment and become owners. With even more financial flexibility, the principle of shared ownership was then expanded to public participation corporations (Hansmann and Kraakman 2000).[8] Even such phenomena profoundly identified with the sharing economy as crowdfunding have existed before. For example, in the guilds in China (Morse 1909) and Europe (Epstein and Prak 2008) as well as among small- and medium-sized enterprises in North America and German-speaking Europe (Winker 1996), it was usual for businesses to lend money to each other, even forming financial vehicles that resemble investment funds. With respect to finance, the sharing economy does not revolutionize. To the contrary, it expands instruments that have been known and practiced for a long time.

Preference for access over ownership? This is also a very established driver. Many people rent flats and cars. The reason is that they either do not have enough means to buy the asset, or the asset is needed only for a short term or that they just prefer to use the asset and not to maintain it. In any case, access over ownership is a common preference in many societies. Columbus leased the ships he travelled in as much as most people choose to pay for access to a taxicab and not for its ownership. Indeed, economic interaction often presupposes second- and third-party ownership. If I want to buy an apple, I don't want to own a supermarket. I presuppose ownership of a supermarket by a person often unknown to me in order to be able to access the apple I want to buy. Preference for access is an arrived idea in economics. What might be happening with the 'sharing economy' is that accessibility is being broadened to more goods, for example, eating in other people's homes (instead of restaurants), sleeping in other people's beds (instead of in hotels, hostels and bed and breakfasts – which were themselves at the forefront of the sharing economy), using other people's infrastructure (for example, cars, trucks, inventory) and so on. But all these examples and counter-examples show that it is not a question of novelty, but one of scale.

On the other hand, technological drivers might have pushed the economic aspects of the sharing economy to another level. The technological drivers identified above were: social networking; mobile and devices platform; and e- or online payment systems. The question of their novelty has at least two aspects. First, are they technological innovations? Here, the answer should be yes. But the second question is whether these technological innovations changed the economics behind the economic drivers mentioned above. And to this second question the answer might be no. The economics of selling unused or underused capacity did not change; neither did the idea of sharing risks, endeavors and responsibility. But it became much easier to offer these opportunities for entrepreneurial actions as it became much easier to scale the opportunities to cooperate, to learn and to access enterprises and entrepreneurs. So, it is not the economics that changed with the sharing economy, but it is technological innovation that gave speed and scale to the dispersion of typically economic ways for individuals and groups to pursue their subjective preferences, to minimize their subjective costs and to learn from themselves and from others in the market process.

It has been mentioned before that there is not so much consensus about the societal drivers of the sharing economy. Or even, there is no consensus whether there are any societal drivers at all. Increasing population density, drive for sustainability, desire for community, and generational altruism were mentioned as some elements that analysts might consider. It is very difficult to assess whether a drive for sustainability; desire for community; and generational altruism really exist. The reason is that contrary to population density, these three are extremely difficult to identify and even more difficult to conceptualize or measure. Population density can explain why there is optimization in the use of resources: if the buying price is lower than the cost of maintaining a resource, it makes sense to buy it. If population density raises the cost of maintenance, the more density increases, the more individuals will generally prefer to pay for access rather than ownership. This reaction to population density often also increases the efficiency of how resources are employed. But there is no logical bridge (let alone a rule) from here to admitting that the 'sharing economy' leads to a more sustainable way of life or that sustainability drives the sharing economy. Some individuals might be incentivized to travel more because of Airbnb or Uber; others might be incentivized to cook or eat more because of Mixxta (Share a table) and the like. Similar problems of identification also apply to the so-called longing for community or in intergenerational solidarity, if they even exist. There is no logical connection between them and the sharing economy. But examples in which the sharing economy could be contrary to these supposed drivers are abundant (Hamaria et al. 2015; Möhlmann 2015).

There is, however, a different way of assessing the role of societal drivers in the sharing economy. The individual or the groups involved in the sharing economy have different subjective preferences, including preferences for values. Some will hold sustainability, solidarity and community as important goals in their lives, and they might employ different instruments facilitated by the sharing economy to fulfill their goals. Maybe even it is easier for these individuals and groups to fulfill their goals of sustainability, solidarity and community in the sharing economy – but this has still to be shown. But here, the cause and effect are the opposite from the claim that sustainability and solidarity drive the sharing economy. It is the sharing economy that makes it easier for some people to pursue solidarity and a sustainable lifestyle. As it is the sharing economy that makes it cheaper for those wanting to experience more, travel more and consume more. Unsurprisingly, this is commensurate with traditional economics. It is not the market processes that tell individuals what to do. The market processes enable and facilitate individuals to pursue their own goals.

1.2.3   Essentialism and Pragmatism

Is the sharing economy something novel or not? Those that answer 'yes' often have the tendency to combine their perception of the novelty of the sharing economy with some essentialist claim about it. One example of such a claim would be: the sharing economy is something completely new that revolutionizes the way people act in the markets. Markets fail most of the time. People do not accept these market failures anymore. That is why they turn to more equitable relations with each other. The sharing economy is a reaction to market failures.

This argument can be countered by the second example of a novelty-cum-essentialist claim: the sharing economy is something new that revolutionizes the exposure of people to power. It breaks the power of regulation and gives back power to the individuals in the markets. By engaging in largely unregulated market processes, people escape the grip of regulation, but also constantly challenge any other convergence of power that might arise in the market. The sharing economy is about making the economy more democratic by the unhindered application of market principles to every human action.

Essentialist claims – either the one or the other – are always problematic because they assume several necessary conditions. As it is not necessarily so that markets fail, it is not necessarily so that market agents always disprove of market power. It is not necessarily so that individuals dislike all types of markets, and it is not necessarily so that people, in order to have individual power over relations, turn to markets. Besides these claims of necessity, some of the implications of the two examples are simply contradictory. If markets fail, why do people turn to a form of the market called the sharing economy? What is there that prevents this market from also failing? And with relation to the second claim, if people do not want market power, why did Uber emerge with such a massive power in the market processes?

Much more in line with the understanding of economics outlined in the first section is denying the novelty of the sharing economy. Its economics is the same as the economics of all other series of exchanges. What is different about it is accelerated pace, diminished costs of operationalization and easier learning effects through technology. If conceptualized in such a way, the sharing economy is nothing more – but also nothing less – than a pragmatic arrangement of individuals or groups to a changed or improved technological environment. As a pragmatic arrangement, the sharing economy is in constant flux about which business models it entails, about their results and about its further development. After all, the sharing economy consists of many different series of exchanges in open-ended, undetermined market processes. Those individuals that first combined their business models with the new opportunities created by technology were not meaning to change the foundation of economic exchange. To the contrary, they were taking advantage of a moment. And the advantage they wanted to take presupposes market processes and their economic foundations.

1.3 THE CASE OF UBER: IS UBER PART OF THE SHARING ECONOMY?

It is now time to focus on Uber. As any entrepreneur would do, the individuals behind Uber seized an opportunity by engaging in a series of market exchanges. Some of these exchanges were about mobilizing financing of the enterprise; others were about organizing technology and expertise. Similarly, Uber acted in the market processes of acquiring labor, customers and suppliers and so on. So far, from the economics behind Uber nothing more special than the action of individual agents in the market processes stands out. The one special element of Uber, at least as it began, was the conscious decision not to buy any cars, but to look for partners with their cars and bring their idle capacity into a network. This is what may be called the differentiator in Uber's idea. While from a managerial and business point of view this is a good idea because it diminishes the amount of assets and the costs related to their maintenance and amortization (and cuts labor costs too), from a purely economic point of view, there is nothing revolutionary about it. This means this business model does not change the economics at all. In fact, it further shows that the Misesian idea of entrepreneurs seizing an opportunity is a good fit to describe these actions.

Connecting partners who at their own risk and with their own assets become part of a network is a 'good' idea since it tends to diminish the costs for all involved, including consumers, and raises opportunities and gains for all, including for the partners. Similar ideas have been applied before Uber, for example, many 'shop in shop' or 'rack jobber' concepts in retail or contract manufacturing.[9] This does not diminish in any way Uber's entrepreneurship. But at the same time puts it into perspective. So, Uber and its founders acted pretty much as the usual agents in the market processes, trying to seize opportunities, acting according to their beliefs, preferences and costs. Uber does not know if it will emerge successfully in the processes it takes part in; also, its financiers, employees and partners do not know any outcomes before they happen. But these individuals' subjective calculations made them join together on a journey of cooperative practices. Simply put, this is the economics of Uber.

Then, there is a question about Uber's relationship to the sharing economy. Some think of Uber as the most important example of the sharing economy. But, as seen above, there is nothing in the sharing economy that sets it fundamentally apart from other ways of exchanging in the market processes. In this case, Uber is not an archetype for anything. It is just a successful company. Others do not consider Uber a part of the sharing economy at all. Let's assume, for the sake of argument, that there is anything defining the sharing economy: why shouldn't Uber belong to it? One argument that is often offered is that Uber makes profits. First, Uber aims at making profit but so far has not reported any (see Chapter 2). Second, most definitions of the sharing economy accept that its agents might seek profits – Botsman (2015) certainly does. Third, and this is the main problem, this argument would not accept any company, probably no one as an agent in the sharing economy, since sharing epistemically presupposes some sort of gain. People only share if they have a preference for it and any preference involves expected utility and gain – albeit not necessarily a monetary gain.

But there is a more sophisticated argument against counting Uber as an agent in the sharing economy. If driver Farook is travelling from Hayward to Sausalito and offers the remaining three seats in his car, he is sharing. If driver Maria waits for people to tell her where to drive to, she is not sharing. But this argument, too, has fallacies. First, it is overly strict with the term 'share.' Share might denote the act of sharing a ride or the fact of sharing an asset, in this case a car. The word sharing is open to both; there are no inherent criteria in its semantics to understand it, only in a limited way of sharing a ride. Second, this argument might work – but it does not – for sorting Uber out of the sharing economy, but does not do justice to others, such as Airbnb, for example. Does the overly strict share argument imply that Gezim has to stay in his apartment if he wants to offer a room to a stranger? Also, Gezim might only incur very small marginal costs by having Fatima staying with him. Does that definition of sharing mean that he is not supposed to charge Fatima more than the marginal costs?

In any case, trying to portray Uber as something potentially outside the sharing economy leads to overly ambitious claims about what the sharing economy is supposed to be – or even allowed to be. No definition about dynamic human actions has this kind of epistemic and binding power. But then again, this discussion offers further plausibility for the view championed in this book. There is no overarching economic phenomenon called the sharing economy. There are business models that rely on networking and selling – or auctioning – idle capacity to customers. These models rely on the market processes, and they especially rely on a higher-paced, learning-intensive market process, that has been facilitated by technology. Uber is a good case for that.

This case merits a deeper appreciation. The next chapter provides an overview on Uber's business model and the entrepreneurship that underlies it. As such, while this chapter provides background to the thinking of this book, the next chapter builds the base for treating Uber as a case study in creative destruction and disruptive innovation.

SUMMARY

The chapter provides the background on the economics of this book, on the 'sharing economy' and how Uber can be assessed as an economic agent. This book understands markets as open-ended undetermined series of exchanges between a potentially unlimited number of agents. These agents engage voluntarily in the different market processes without knowing more than the other agents but judging their own beliefs, preferences and costs subjectively. Agents use the market processes in order to learn about other agents' beliefs, preferences and costs. Market processes are cooperative actions.

Whatever might be labelled the sharing economy relies on these market processes and does not in any way fundamentally change them. The sharing economy is not different from the traditional economy; to the contrary, it applies and broadens the application of market processes and individual actions. However, the role that technology plays is important. With the development of online networking, e- and online payment methods as well as individual online mobility, many business models gain scale and scope. Technology often makes it possible to diminish costs of participating in a market process, to learn quickly or gather information in a timely manner as well as to scale up some market processes. Uber, in due entrepreneurial spirit, seized this opportunity and turned it into a successful business model.

NOTES

1. *Weltanschauung* is the exact German word for worldview. However, it is often used in English with a philosophical content. It refers to the frame of reference of the subject; the ideas and beliefs upon which a person watches and interprets the world with which he interacts.
2. In his book *The Construction of Social Reality* (Searle 1995) and later works, John Searle discusses the problem that 'there are portions of the real world, objective facts in the world, that are only facts by human agreement' (p. 42). He describes these objective facts as observer relative features of reality, or components of 'social reality,' as opposed to the intrinsic features of physical reality or 'brute facts,' such as rocks, water and trees. He then asks the question, 'how is a socially constructed reality possible?' and devotes much of this book to providing some answers. According to him, most social entities emerge from cooperative practices, especially cooperative linguistic practices.
3. The philosopher Ludwig Wittgenstein (1889–1951) coined this term. It denotes similar things that are connected not through any one essential common feature, but by many or a series of overlapping similarities. Wittgenstein's paradigmatic example was the one of games: soccer, darts, Warcraft do not share one and only essential and necessary criterion, but they are all called games. They are common social practices that are best referred to as games, even if a player of Warcraft never watched or heard of soccer before. The idea of

family resemblance is present in much of Wittgenstein's work, but the most detailed explanation is found in his *Philosophische Untersuchungen* [*Philosophical Investigations*] (1945).

4. Think, for example, of the financial markets and the Fed's interest rates. Most agents in the financial markets do not want an interest rate hike. These agents are part of the economy. Some right-wing political tendencies accept the maxim that the state should do what's possible to help the economy ('jumpstarting the economy' argument). By that maxim it would mean the Fed should not raise interest rates. Austrian economics, for example, postulates that interest rates are the price of money. An entity like the Fed keeping them deliberately and artificially low distorts the whole of the economy because it changes prices. Another example is that many sectors of the economy demand some sort of subsidy. Sectors traditionally associated with right-wing politics profit from subsidies, for example, defense industry or agriculture. Austrian economics is skeptical of all forms of subsidies because they distort the individual, subjective calculations of utility and cost.

5. The appropriateness of reading a given theory can be achieved by applying Davidson's principle of charity: the basic problem that radical interpretation must address is that one cannot assign meanings to a speaker's utterances without knowing what the speaker believes, while one cannot identify beliefs without knowing what the speaker's utterances mean. It seems that we must provide both a theory of belief and a theory of meaning at one and the same time. Davidson claims that the way to achieve this is through the application of the so-called 'principle of charity' (Davidson has also referred to it as the principle of 'rational accommodation'), a version of which is also to be found in Quine. In Davidson's work this principle, which admits to various formulations and cannot be rendered in any completely precise form, often appears in terms of the injunction to optimize agreement between ourselves and those we interpret, that is, it counsels us to interpret speakers as holding true beliefs (true by our lights at least) wherever it is plausible to do (Davidson 1973). In the case of this book, it evaluates these authors and their theories in the same background they have been developed.

6. Besides these objections grounded in the institutional view of markets, there are many other ways to challenge the market as optimal equilibrium view. Just take a look at the assumptions that theory has to make in order to work: (a) a set of perfectly competitive markets exists for inputs and outputs; (b) each market has an equilibrium price; (c) equilibrium prices clear the markets; (d) zero transaction costs; (e) perfect knowledge; (f) no transportation costs; (g) the Law of One Price – each good and input obeys this law, which is that the good or input is homogeneous and sells for the same price to everyone in all markets; (h) all consumers are rational price takers both as buyers of goods and sellers of inputs (for example, labor). Each market has a very large number of utility-maximizing consumers for any one good or input; (i) all firms are rational price takers in both input and output markets. Each market has a very large number of profit-maximizing firms producing each homogeneous good or input.

7. Ockham's razor, or the law of briefness, was developed by the fourteenth-century Franciscan friar William of Ockham (1285–1347). Its original formulation was in Latin and can be translated as 'More things should not be used than are necessary.' Often, the razor is understood as a common sense principle saying that the simplest explanation is usually the right one. Ockham, however, was trying to formulate a scientific principle for settling the question of who bears the burden of proof, for example, when claiming that Nature has a Will of its own, or a stone flies because it wants to fly. The razor tells us that if I claim that the stone flies because it wants to fly, it is my responsibility to prove it wanting to fly. If I also claim that the stone flies because I threw it, I would have to prove that too. The simplest proof, then, is the more adequate. Ockham himself also championed other causes like the freedom of the individual, the unconditionality of private property or the privilege of intention over reason. Because of his rather revolutionary thought, he was excommunicated from the Catholic Church (Keele 2010).

8. It is a matter for historians to say which was the first shared entrepreneurship company in history. Some claim it was the Banco di San Giorgio founded in 1407 in Genoa; others say it was the Vereenigde Oostindische Compagnie (Dutch East India Company) founded in 1602.

9. The shop in shop retail concept is where a brand owner or retailer takes space in another retailer's store and fits it out to provide selling space dedicated to that secondary company's products. Rack jobbing occurs when a wholesaler provides racks of merchandise for retail locations and the wholesaler and the retailer split the profits obtained from sales between the two parties. Convenience stores are often made up of various rack jobbers from large and small wholesalers. Contracted manufacturing is the case when the production of goods by one firm is under the label or brand of another firm. Contract manufacturers provide such a service to several (even competing) firms based on their own or the customers' designs, formulas and/or specifications.

2. What is Uber's business model?

'Cutting out the middleman.' No. That is not Uber's business model. In fact, it is quite its contrary. Uber re-intermediates the taxicab market. This is especially counter-intuitive, since the taxicab industry has been working without middlemen for a long time. And usually, intermediaries are cost-drivers that most market processes want to avoid or to eliminate (Katz 1988, p. 32).

For some economists, intermediaries as such are a problem. For example, Akerlof in his seminal article, 'The market for lemons' (1970) claims that intermediaries have a perverse incentive to be dishonest. They have more information than the other agents in the market processes and therefore can use this to their advantage. For example, a salesperson could lie to a customer when selling a used car because no matter what, the salesperson knows more about that particular car than the customer will ever know before buying it. So, why not sell a car full of problems, a lemon, to the little-knowing customer? That is the general pre-occupation of Akerlof. How does he propose to solve the problem? By regulating the middlemen.[1]

But then there is yet another economic intuition. It is the one calling for specialization. No economic agent is fully self-sufficient, for example, in growing all his food or producing all his clothing, constructing all of her house or manufacturing her entire car. Instead, most people rely on the market processes to fulfill their desires at the cost they are prepared to pay. Sometimes, agents in the market even want an intermediary, someone that deals with information. If that were not the case, there would be no newspapers, teachers or even books, for these are all intermediaries, or dealers of information. The real questions are how do market agents develop trust toward these dealers of information and how much are they willing to pay for their services? An economy with specialization presupposes, therefore, some amount of intermediation and with that some asymmetry of information. Less surprisingly put, the price for specialization is information asymmetry.

Uber, using a technology that allows a quicker, often more transparent flow of information, succeeded in establishing itself as a specialized intermediary in at least two senses. The one sense of intermediation is instead of customers directly calling a taxicab company or a single taxi, they use Uber's app. In order to do so, they reveal vital information about themselves. Examples are their telephone or credit card number. In return, they are allowed access to two types of information that only Uber provides, or at least provided as it entered the market: the location of vehicles and the rating of drivers.

In the second sense of intermediation, Uber aggregates information about the suppliers of transportation, that is, the drivers. These drivers could have opted for marketing their services directly to the consumers, but instead they agree to offer them through the intermediary Uber. There are different reasons for their decision, for example, advertising, profiting from the network effect, accessing technology or not being regulated. But these drivers also pay a price for Uber's intermediation, if not in money, then in behavior. They, too, have to adapt to the intermediary's policies, for example, to its pricing, to its rating system or to its surveillance methods.

Is that, then, Uber's business model? Intermediation? No, it is not. But intermediation certainly is a facet among many, and perhaps the most counter-intuitive one. Normally, re-intermediating a sector is not a successful recipe for market penetration. However, in Uber's case it is, because it is also the most cost-effective way to scale up the selling of excess capacity. And it is the most cost-effective way of doing so because it relies almost entirely on information technology. These three elements together – intermediation, allowing access to idling capacity and technology – together with a peculiar definition of transparency, some marketing and the negative perception of the taxicab industry at large, explain Uber's success.

But there is more to Uber than this last paragraph summarizes. This chapter investigates Uber's business model, the entrepreneurship behind it and also its specific differences toward the traditional taxicab industry. The leading question of this chapter does not call for a complete description of all the intricacies of Uber. But it warrants a discussion about what makes Uber innovative, thus preparing the case study about Uber's disruptive force and it being brought to a halt by regulation – which is at the core of Chapters 3 and 4. In order to understand the novelty of Uber's business model, however, some contextualization is needed; through a brief history of the taxicab industry that is also the history of its regulation. As in the previous chapter, a general framework is first developed and then this framework is applied to Uber. The third section of the chapter discusses what the 'Uberization' or the 'Uberification' of an economy might be. The summary answers the leading question of this chapter: what is Uber's business model?

2.1 OF TAXICABS AND STRATEGIES

For many contemporary users, taxicabs and strategy might not seem a natural fit. However, history shows that the taxicab industry has an interesting past marked by innovation, dynamic strategies and even challenging the views of officialdom. What is today perceived as an industry following a strategy – if any – of regulation and cartelization was once known for innovation. Taxicabs were once even at the technological vanguard of their time. Uber's relative success is due to many factors, but chiefly among them is the loss of innovative pace in the traditional taxicab industry. This section traces the taxicab and its regulation back in time and introduces the concept of strategy in the contemporary sense.

2.1.1 A Short History of Taxicabs

The commercial transportation of passengers, and its regulation, goes back centuries. Horse-drawn coaches-for-hire first appeared on the streets of Paris and London in the early seventeenth century. These independent operators were unregulated and literally freewheeling (Harris 2010). The symbolism of that trade should not be underestimated: in a time in which only people from the upper classes were able to use their private carriages and coaches for transportation, expanding this possibility to other people, commoners, was at least mildly radical. Because of their success with the public, the number of these coaches-for-hire grew rapidly. King Charles I of England[2] wanted at first to forbid these coaches, but he conceded then in regulating them. In 1635 a royal order demanded their regulation and licensing. Similar was the development of the first taxis in most European capitals, especially Vienna, Madrid and St Petersburg (Harris 2010).[3]

In the nineteenth century, a new model of carriage revolutionized the taxicab industry. Architect Joseph Hansom[4] patented the Hansom cab in 1834. This two-wheel vehicle was fast, light enough to be pulled by a single horse and flexible enough to tour narrow allies. Being able to be pulled by just one horse was the main technological innovation of the Hansom cab. One horse was less than the usual two that were needed and that meant lower costs, lower prices and more supply. London in the nineteenth century suffered from severe traffic jams, so having a vehicle flexible enough to maneuver through the traffic as well as use alternative routes was another advantage. It was the Hansom cab that arrived in New York by the end of that century. Hansom cabs also underwent a further technological innovation that has been forgotten and is only slowly returning today: they were modified to run on electricity. The so-called 'Hummingbirds' were not only affordable and quick vehicles running on the streets of London and New York, they were also fully powered by electricity (Harris 2010).

Parallel to all of this, in Germany, where taxicabs were also heavily regulated – much like all of that country's economy – motorized cars and the taximeter were invented. Gottlieb Daimler[5] introduced the motorized and taxi-metered cab, the 'Victoria,' in the city of Stuttgart in 1897. Harry N. Allen brought one of these models to New York in 1907. Because these vehicles were cheaper than the electrical Hummingbird and could cover larger rides – New York City is a vast city – they became the vehicle of choice. The taximeter fulfilled a promise of transparency and objectivity, immediately winning the public's sympathies. But Allen's success was not only based on a good vehicle with transparent pricing. Much like Uber, Allen needed heavy financing for his endeavor. He relied on his father, who was a stockbroker, and on the newspaper magnate William Randolph Hearst[6] investing in his company. He needed a larger fleet in order to capitalize on scale. And Allen needed marketing. One of his first approaches in marketing has marked the whole industry forever since. In order to make his taxicab visible, he decided to paint all the vehicles the same color: yellow.

Allen, too, had to deal with different difficulties that had arisen out of his novel business model. The company owned the cars, but the drivers were largely self-employed. As such, they had to pay for their own uniforms, they had to polish the brass of their vehicles and, most importantly, they had to pay for gasoline themselves. Why would someone under these circumstances become a driver for Allen? To escape unemployment or menial work. Keep in mind that it was the time of massive population inflow in New York City. The drivers' costs amounted to about 1.20 dollars per day but, on the other hand, they could charge 5 dollars for a three-quarter mile trip in Manhattan. And the drivers could keep 1 percent of what they made. This perspective of profit did not seem to fulfill the drivers' wishes. Instead, they demanded a flat salary of 2.5 dollars per day. In order to obtain that, they went on strike (Hodges 2009).

In addition, many of the other taxicab companies of that time were opposed to Allen's large fleet of gasoline-powered yellow cars. They claimed that Allen was engaging in unfair competition, uncivilized business practices and even moral decay. Their rage was further fuelled by Allen himself who liked seeing his fleet parading Manhattan's avenues. This was his way of advertising the comfort offered by his business model, implicitly showing how uncomfortable the other cabs were. In the end, they settled. The older technologies were driven out of the market anyway and Allen made deals with his drivers, offering them flat salaries and pension plans. The competition with other taxi companies would remain – at least for a while (Hodges 2009).

In the 1920s, John Daniel Hertz, a Slovakian-born amateur boxer, horse breeder and car salesman in Chicago, introduced the taxicab to that city and also set up companies in New York and other places. Hertz even expanded the company-wide social safety net for his drivers: he instituted profit sharing with workers, and kept a doctor, dentist and nurse on staff to service them. But Hertz also reduced the prices of taxiing, making taxis affordable to the middle class. As he promised to respond to service calls within ten minutes, he also increased service levels. Lower prices, quicker service and a good understanding with his workers did not bring Hertz only advantages. Yes, he had quickly risen to the country's largest fleet. And yes, he had the biggest market share. But he was also reviled by other taxi companies and sometimes there were even shootings among taxi drivers of different companies (Hodges 2009).

As Allen had innovated in bringing a new form of technology (gasoline and taximeter) as well as a new form of advertising (yellow cab) to the United States, Hertz innovated by introducing scale (by having the largest fleet), lowering prices and increasing quality. Hertz did not rest. He still tried to innovate more. His intuition told him that prices could be lowered even further, for example, by eliminating the driver. That is how the 'Hertz Drive-Ur-Self Corporation' was born – and that is how the name Hertz is still widely known today.

In the times of Allen and Hertz, the taxicab industry was not as strictly regulated as it is today. Some safety standards applied and some labor regulations had to be met. But such things as who could offer cab services or at what price they could be offered were largely left to the entrepreneur's and their customers' discretion. It was for the market processes to find these things out. Indeed, only because of the flexibility was Hertz able to capitalize on scale – more units of a good or a service can be produced on a larger scale, yet with on average less input costs – lowering the prices and increasing the quality of employment. But that was soon to change.

Before the Great Depression of the 1930s, there were some 84,000 taxi drivers in the United States. By 1932 that number had gone up to about 150,000. Because of the Great Depression, the number of cars for hire exploded, since people who had been let go in other companies opened taxicab businesses. Complaints about taxicabs clogging the streets, uninsured drivers regularly getting into accidents that injured passengers and unsavory drivers engaging in criminal activities made the rounds in the press and this led to political pressure in favor of more regulation. New York City's Board of Aldermen, then with a Republican majority (the predecessor of the modern New York City Council), responded to calls for regulation in 1937 by passing the Haas Act. The Haas Act established the medallion system for New York taxicabs, which is still in use today. The Act's provisions included a limitation on the number of medallion licenses (and therefore, taxicabs) to the number that existed at the time. This number would be further reduced. As anticipated, this measure calmed the fierce competition for customers. It also curbed innovation. On the other hand, the stability the Haas Act brought to the taxi industry laid the foundation for the later 'success' (that is, the stability of taxicab firms, their steady gains from monopoly and so on) of the war and post-war years.

Not only regulation, but a singular amalgamation of post-Depression events helped the taxi industry in New York thrive. Facing the rationing of fuel and car parts during World War II, many turned to taxis for transportation. The resulting jump in demand helped the taxi industry grow, as drivers no longer had to fight for business. Meanwhile, the value of medallions increased exponentially once license holders realized that they were indeed a transferable asset somewhat like real estate. While licenses were sold at 10 dollars in 1937, medallions traded for an average 5,000 dollars in 1950. By May 2013, these medallions reached their peak price, about 1.32 million dollars. Today, a medallion can be bought at a price slightly above 600,000 dollars. Why did prices fall? Because of the market entry of Uber and others (Schneider 2015).

Developments in Europe and other regions were not completely different. The US system of taxi medallions regulates the maximum quantity of taxicab capacity. As this capacity becomes scarce, its price rises. The alternative is practiced in Europe, where licenses are issued. A license has a price set by a regulator, that is, it is not determined in auction or by any other market mechanism. But the regulator only issues the new licenses it considers necessary to fulfill the expectation of demand and supply for transportation in its legislation. Also, the regulator closely scrutinizes the qualifications either of the taxicab company or the drivers personally; often, both of them. In many European nations, regulators also divide markets among taxicab companies, for example, by stipulating monopolies in return for servicing a low-frequency region (see, for example, Listl and Dammann 2009).

As suggested above, however, the price for the so-called success of the taxicab industry was high. The taxicab industry became heavy cartelized with extremely high market entrance barriers. Taxis were impeded in competing over price since all tariffs were fixed and capped. Also, there was no competition over quality since even the exact car models allowed for taxiing were regulated. Taxi companies became less and less entrepreneurial. From the introduction of the Haas Act until the market entry of Uber, there was no innovation in the taxicab industry. Neither pricing models nor advertisement. It was like a freeze in space-time. And this explains why sometimes taxicab and strategy are perceived as contradictions.

What is there to learn from this brief history of the taxicab industry? Even if the focus of the second part of the subsection is New York City, its learnings can be generalized. Taxicabs, as any other industry, develop over time. Enterprises adapt their business model to the general conditions of the societies in which they operate. But now and then, some entrepreneur will take advantage of the opportunities and introduce novelties. Indeed, the history of taxicabs seems to show that innovation was the rule, at least for a long time. But this same history shows that regulation was never very far from the reality of the taxicab business. This history shows that regulating taxicabs usually followed different rationales. If class distinction was its first preoccupation, preventing oversupply soon took over as chief motivation. Other rationales were and are the security of customers and employees. In order to understand the specific difference of Uber, it is useful to take a quick look at these rationales.

2.1.2   Rationales of Regulation

While Chapter 4 examines the economic rationale of taxicab regulations in detail, this subsection provides an overview on how different arguments for regulation emerged in the most recent history of taxicabs. As mentioned above, in the 1930s political groups claimed that unregulated taxicabs led to traffic jams, predatory pricing and injuries to customers or even to crime. The academic literature on why taxicabs should be regulated nuances these reasons, and finds them mostly correct.

From the beginning, the so-called oversupply of taxicabs was the main justification for regulation (Wyman 2013). The crude argument is that since driving a taxicab does not require extensive qualification, the costs of market entry are too low. (Note how this claim presupposes an objective measure of what that cost might or should be.) This bears the danger of virtually anyone becoming a driver, turning this sector thus into a catch basin for the unskilled. Economists trusting the market process might perceive this as something positive. If there is a chance even for the most unskilled to make an entrepreneurial living – why should it be not regarded as an opportunity? However, if markets are seen from an institutional point of view, stipulating the rules for entering a market is almost as constitutive to the market-as-institution as the behavior of its agents. In this view, if all other markets presuppose qualification regulated by government, no exceptions for the taxicabs can be made.

There are two or three more sophisticated arguments. First, there is the claim that the roads of a city are a common good. A common good benefits society as a whole, in contrast to the private good of individuals and sections of society. Since taxicabs are using a common good for their own profit, there should be some limit to how much of that common good they are allowed to use. The second sophisticated argument uses the concept of negative externalities. A negative externality occurs when an individual or firm making a decision does not have to pay the full cost of the decision. If a good has a negative externality, then the cost to society is greater than the cost the consumer is paying for it. So, if taxicabs charge their customers to drive them, they neither bear nor charge the cost of creating or contributing to traffic jams. Also, if taxicab drivers take advantage of their customers, it is either the customer or society that pays for the restitution of the damage. In this logic, since taxicab companies are not imputing all the costs of their behavior to their costs and prices, they should be regulated. The third sophisticated argument is based on information asymmetry. Information asymmetry is the fact that many aspects of the taxi service cannot be examined by customers prior to consumption. Thus, it is doubtful whether taxi consumers possess the information on price and service offerings needed to establish a truly competitive market. The same asymmetry applies to the drivers. These economists really think that 'ignorance of true market conditions and lack of alternative employment opportunities may lead to persistent oversupply' (Wyman 2013).

It is remarkable how a shift from the main motivation to the sophisticated arguments occur. While the main idea was to curb oversupply making it more difficult or more expensive for newcomers to enter into this market, the arguments turn to institutions of last resort, like the greater good of society. This is important for the regulatory logic. It is in this standpoint of the greater good of society that regulators ground the claim for having an objective measure of what augments that greater good and what diminishes it. That is why regulators usually endorse institutional views of markets, in which there are ideal configurations of prices and quantity and objective measures for the state of those markets. In the market processes view, however, objective measures and ideal configurations of the greater good of society do not exist, since the states of the market processes are judged individually and subjectively by the agents in these processes.

If markets are understood as processes, many of these regulatory preoccupations are problematic. It is safe to assume that drivers and customers will be interested in acquiring more information before deciding. An individual consumer might even accept a higher price, if this higher price reduces the costs of gathering information. In any case, how much time anyone wants to devote in navigating information is a subjective decision. The same subjectivity applies to the drivers and other businesspeople: it does not seem realistic that a person makes a decision on what job or entrepreneurial activity to pursue without getting all the information it considers necessary. Arguing that individuals become taxicab drivers out of ignorance about costs and alternatives is a difficult argument to construct. It is just as difficult as sustaining the idea of the roads as a common good and the application of negative externalities to taxicabs. Taxicab drivers pay taxes and tolls for maintaining and building roads just like other vehicles. They are not contributing more to traffic jams than others; if anything, they contribute less because they make it possible for a vehicle to be used by multiple people. And taxicab companies know, just as any other company, that they can be sued for damages. There is no taxi-specific damage that is not covered by the general body of law. Most of these regulatory preoccupations reveal some distrust toward the market processes. They also reveal the intention of finding so-called solutions under pretexts that often bear little significance. This thinking has remained almost unchallenged for the last 70 years.

And then Uber entered the market. As Uber began, it had neither a medallion nor a license, since it considered itself a technology company, or a matchmaker platform and not a transportation business. The thrust of the controversy facing Uber is whether the legal definition of a taxi and limousine includes an operator such that it 'only' provides a reservation arrangement service to customers. Uber does not employ cars and drivers. However, given the investments of taxi and limousine drivers to maintain a medallion, registrations and chauffeur licenses, they are inherently threatened and in opposition to any new entrants that have the potential to absorb a share of riders. The regulatory question about the character of Uber can be answered in two different ways. If the criterion is its customers, Uber is a provider of transportation just like taxicabs and limousine services. If the criterion is the product as such, that is, the service, then Uber, at least in its initial form, is not comparable to the other agents of the taxicab industry. Which criterion applies is a political decision.

The last sentence of the previous paragraph might seem a consensual, perhaps wise, way of settling the dispute. However, as will be shown in Chapter 4, it makes it even more difficult: a matter of economic theory is turned into a matter of regulation. And a matter of regulation becomes a political deliberation. And with each step along this chain, it becomes more complicated and – which is important – least feasible from the economic point of view. Chapter 4 is mostly concentrated on the assessment of the adequacy of regulation. For the aims of this chapter, it is important to see how regulation influenced Uber's strategy since its beginning. Even in the United States.

For example, to protest Uber's entry into Washington DC's market, the local taxicab companies arranged a 'sting' in January 2012 to impound and ticket Uber's drivers. The account of this episode was given by the *Washington Post*:

> An Uber car was impounded and its driver was ticketed this morning as part of a sting operation, said the [DC taxicab] commission chairman, Ron Linton. The action comes two days after Linton said in a commission meeting that he considered the service to be operating illegally. Linton played a key role in the morning sting, hailing a car using Uber's smartphone app then directing it to the Mayflower Hotel, where city hack inspectors were waiting. The driver … was ticketed for four violations – not holding a chauffeur license, driving an unlicensed vehicle, not having proof of insurance and charging an improper fare. The violations carry combined fines of $1,650 … 'What they're trying to do is be both a taxi and a limousine,' Linton said. 'Under the way the law is written, it just can't be done.'[7]

Uber has also faced challenges in its home market of San Francisco and was forced to respond to a cease-and-desist order as early as 2010. In this instance, Uber was scrutinized when it originally advertised the company as 'Uber Taxi,' while none of its drivers possess a taxi medallion required to operate as a taxi in San Francisco.[8] Since this incident, Uber has modified its company name to a shortened 'Uber,' and is continuing to grow in San Francisco. However, the cease-and-desist order was a reminder of the stringent regional taxi and limousine laws. Uber also came under close scrutiny in Asia and Europe in particular. Uber has even been banned from markets like the city of Paris in France or the state (canton) of Geneva in Switzerland, a country commonly known as a free economy. It will be a matter for Chapters 3 and 4 to show how Uber constantly changed its business model in order to face regulation. However, as seen here, regulation conflicted with Uber's strategy from the beginning.

2.1.3 Startup and Strategy

In Chapter 1 it was stated that agents engage in the market processes in order to fulfill their preferences at costs they can bear. In the last two subsections it has been shown that different types of entrepreneurs adopted unique strategies in the taxicab industry. The strategic innovation in that sector came to a halt because of regulation. This type of statement calls for at least a brief definition of strategy and how it relates to the market process outlined previously.

Business theorists claim that every company needs a strategy. No matter if a conglomerate behemoth or a startup in a garage, without a strategy no firm knows which direction to take. Johnson et al. (2008, p. 25) define strategy as follows: 'Strategy is the direction and scope of an organization over the long-term: which achieves advantage for the organization through its configuration of resources within a challenging environment, to meet the needs of markets and to fulfil stakeholder expectations.'

Strategy, then, has to provide answers to questions like: Where is the business trying to get to in the long-term (direction)? Which markets should a business compete in and what kind of activities are involved in such markets (markets, scope)? How can the business perform better than the competition in those markets (advantage)? What resources (skills, assets, finance, relationships, technical competence, facilities) are required in order to be able to compete (resources)? What external, environmental factors affect the businesses' ability to compete (environment)? What are the values and expectations of those who have power in and around the business (stakeholders)?

In order to answer these questions, business strategists have first to analyse the factors that determine the questions above. They especially have to develop different scenarios about how these factors can change. This is elemental because they will change. In the market processes change is the norm. Therefore, no matter which long-run direction of activities a firm chooses, it will have to deal with several short-term changes of directions. As agents in the market processes, companies have to constantly adapt to all the dynamics of these changes. In order to combine a sense of direction and adaptation to the circumstances, companies adopt strategies.

If the agents act in the market processes through constant evaluation of different flows and stocks of information, it is a company's strategy that provides a scale for measuring how these flows and stocks impact the firm's individual preferences and cost structures and therefore evaluating the possible actions and reactions of that firm. In other words, the strategy is the tool for a company to engage in a long-term market process. The business model of a firm, on the other hand, gives that firm a plan on how to use the tool that the strategy is. And this leads directly to the core of this chapter: Uber's business model.

2.2 UBER'S BUSINESS MODEL

Capacity comes at a steady cost, since it has to be maintained. However, most capacity is not used to its full potential. For example, millions of cars, which are a transportation capacity, are standing or being driven without being used to their fullest. The same applies to internet bandwidth, spare rooms or even food. Some entrepreneurs – as they usually do – recognize such business opportunities: what if some of the unused capacity is sold to third parties, that is, customers? This is how Airbnb works; private parties can offer spare rooms in their homes to third parties.

And this is also the idea – at least, at its beginning it was – behind Uber. Private cars that aren't used to their maximum capacity can be rented by third parties, much like a taxicab. This allocation of unused or underused capacity, however, needs intermediation, which tends to be costly. But if the intermediary finds a way to lower the costs of intermediation and at the same time a way for scaling up, it can successfully reach a wide group of consumers and match them to the spare capacity. The technological platform of Uber's app was the way that at the same time allowed for scaling up and diminishing costs. Uber started and defined itself as the technology provider, that is, an intermediary, offering the software needed to match the demand and supply of capacity spots in the private market for locomotion. But this purist definition of itself was about to be changed because of its interaction with regulation. This is why this section portrays Uber's startup business model as it was in 2010. Its subsequent changes will be dealt with in Chapters 3 and 4.

2.2.1 Uber's Strategy

Imagine a triangle formed by the following value propositions, 'cheap,' 'fast,' 'quality' (Foxall 2014). Startups and early movers usually chose one or two of them in order to position themselves. At its start, Uber relied on two value propositions, 'fast' and 'cheap.' It had to be fast in order to attract customers willing to defer from the usual waiting for a cab or standing in line for a taxi and it had to be cheap in order to appeal to the clients' monetary preferences. Note that being cheap does not automatically mean underbidding the others. It can also be achieved by having a simpler and more transparent pricing structure, thus minimizing transaction and information costs. Being cheap also can entail selling a better service level for the price of the competition, for example, riding a limousine for the price of a taxicab – this insight becomes important again in the second section of Chapter 3.

Though the company was founded in 2009, Uber didn't officially launch until June 2010. The initial launch city was San Francisco. The company's founders invested 200,000 dollars as seed money, which is moderate for a technology company. After its initial success and with its continuous expansions, much higher funds were to follow.[9] As of April 2016, the service is available in over 60 countries and 404 cities worldwide (most of this subsection follows Uber's self-declaration and Cohen and Kietzmann 2014).

Uber's initial business model is quite simple. There is a web app, an advanced computer program as well as marketing and public relations. At the intersection of lifestyle and logistics, Uber is a two-sided marketplace of buyers and sellers. The company was supposed to own no inventory, warehouses, distribution centers or other ancillary overhead required for most traditional business models to operate. At its market entrance, Uber was not in the taxi business per se, at least not in the conventional sense, since it owns no cabs and has no cab drivers as employees. Instead, it plays the role of matchmaker, matching a driver/car with a customer looking for a ride. Its value-add comes from the screening that it does of the drivers/cars (to ensure both safety and comfort), its pricing/payment system (where customers choose the level of service, ranging from a car to a limousine, are quoted a fare and pay Uber) and its convenience (where one can track the car that is coming to pick one up on one's phone screen).

An attempt at analysing and systematizing the elements of Uber's business model follows. There are five main elements: (1) Uber's role as a two-sided intermediary; (2) its instruments of intermediation; (3) its technology; (4) its pricing; and (5) its marketing. Each of these main elements has some defining features. They are:[10]

1. Two-sided intermediary: creating networks
    ● *The drivers*: anyone with a car in one of Uber's covered cities can apply to become an Uber driver. If this person passes the internal screenings and assessments, the driver is given the Uber iPhone and becomes a partner in the system. The driver owns the car and proceeds at his own risk, including insurance. It is

the driver that logs in the time and capacity he or she wants to commit. His or her motivations are marketing their idle capacity and higher income relative to traditional taxis.

- *The customers*: Uber subscribers download an app to their phones, register and provide contact details and a valid credit card. In need of a car, the customer enters the app, decides which of the different Uber services to use and then tracks the car as it approaches. After the ride, customers rate the drivers and this rating becomes available to all customers. The customers' motivations are convenience, comfort, some feeling of safety since the price range of the ride is communicated before the ride, transparency about the driver and, sometimes, cost savings in comparison to the traditional taxicab.
- *Intermediating the intermediaries*: Uber also targets other intermediaries in order to offer them its services. For example, Google estimates routes and prices using Uber; or when booking online with Starwood, the customer is automatically prompted with the option of arranging an Uber ride to the booked hotel. The motivation for the other intermediaries is to provide services to their customers and maintain their loyalty.
2. The instruments of intermediation
- *Pricing and payment*: Uber sets the prices for rides, with premium prices for rides during peak demand times (surge pricing, see below). Customers pay Uber for the rides. They don't pay the drivers. Customers also don't tip the drivers. The aim of this element is to guarantee safe and secure transactions to all parties involved, customers, drivers and the intermediary. Before the ride, Uber estimates its price range. After completing the ride, an exact price is calculated. The price depends on distance, car type, service level and demand period.
- *Splitting the proceeds*: Uber splits the ride receipts with the driver. Usually, Uber keeps around 20 percent, an all-in intermediation fee.
- *Revenue and profits*: from the revenues of splitting the proceeds, Uber covers its expenses. These include research and development, technology development, customer acquisition costs, marketing and the employees and infrastructure it needs in order to operate. Uber has a low-cost, no inventory philosophy that allows it to keep a large percentage of revenues either as profits or reinvestments in the firm.
- *Reinvesting in the firm*: Uber needs to reinvest in order to expand. Its low-cost model is only financeable if the scale it

promises to customers and drivers is implemented. This means ultimately that Uber has to aim toward a near complete coverage at least of the world's largest cities and capitals. This might require Uber to acquire local operations, to adapt its software, to adapt its management or to expand its scope. Dealing with regulation does not traditionally fall into the concept of re-investing in the firm. However, in Uber's case it might be. Uber reacted to regulation by changing various propositions of its business plans, for example, by buying vehicles or even paying drivers.

3. Technology
    - *The app:* the app technology is available for iPhone/Android devices and uses the Global Positioning System (GPS) from the requested pickup destination to display a map of all available Uber cars in the area. Uber calculates the nearest driver and plots the pickup time accordingly. Each driver is also given an iPhone with an app to manage incoming customer requests.
    - *Technology at firm level:* the firm employs prediction algorithms and heat maps to predict expected demand at different times of the day. It analyses how many times the app is open and where clusters are located to help manage taxi supply and demand. Another source of operations management is what the firm calls 'God View,' which displays all the active Uber drivers and pending customer requests in real time to ensure quality is maintained on the systems.

4. Pricing
    - Even if quickly out of date, the following examples show Uber's approach to pricing (and its differences to traditional taxicab companies).[11] Uber has three main pricing structures: fixed airport rates; standard fees that include per mile/minute charge; and dynamic pricing. For example, the fixed airport fee from downtown Chicago to Midway airport is 65 dollars and 75 dollars to O'Hare airport, slightly less than two times that of traditional taxicabs. This pricing structure does not differ much from other car services but the convenience factor through the value proposition 'fast' and technology provides it with a competitive edge. The standard Chicago fee, for example, was a base fare of 7.00 dollars plus 3.50 dollars per mile when the vehicle drives over 11 miles per hour and 0.85 dollars when the velocity is less than 11 miles per hour, all calculated using GPS. Customers travelling short distances are subject to the firm's 15 dollars minimum fare as well.[12]

- The pricing structure is about twice the price of cabs in the city but Uber does not charge extra for additional occupants. The pricing structure also leads to an all-electronic payment process. The tip is already included in the final fare and all the customer has to do is keep its credit card information updated with Uber. Again, technology and the value proposition 'fast' provides Uber with a competitive edge. The final and most controversial pricing structure is Uber's use of dynamic pricing for high volume days such as New Year or Halloween and also during inclement weather conditions. During its introductory phases in the different markets, Uber was willing to distribute vouchers for 10 or 20 dollars, thus lowering the paid prices of the rides.
- Note how different aspects come together. Uber's intuition is that early adopters are willing to pay a higher fare for more transparence and less transaction cost as well as in order to achieve the higher service level and escape the hailing and waiting. Also, as a matchmaker allocating unused capacity in a dynamic market, Uber used the forces of demand and supply to determine the market price of the auctioned capacity. As the demanded quantities of taxicabs increase and their supplied quantity decrease during Halloween or a snow storm, so prices rise. This is part of the life-auctioning system that is at the center of capacity allocation.

5. Marketing
   - *Novelty and convenience*: from the beginning, Uber stressed its novelty and convenience in its marketing. Targeting primarily business users in hotels and airports, Uber advertises the superior product and flexible service. Apart from this more or less traditional approach, Uber was quick to form partnerships with other intermediaries (see above). The company successfully uses mass media including Twitter and Facebook to showcase its product and technology websites and blogs have shown an interest in the transportation industry. But one of the most important parts of its marketing, however, was the celebrity endorsement Uber received, which positions its services as hip.[13]
   - *Noisy market entry*: Uber used a 'noisy entry strategy' and technological discontinuity to find a niche in the taxicab market. The company recognized a growing frustration that many customers have with the taxi industry and realized the technical incompetence, or cognitive gap, of incumbent firms. Uber understood the growing market of consumers that use smartphones, which is now estimated to be 80 percent in the United

States and 69 percent in Western Europe, and the fact that early adopters are willing to pay a premium price for convenience, professionalism and cleanliness. The app technology is straightforward and there is a very small learning curve for early adopters to understand the Uber product. Even with a niche customer base of upper class professionals, Uber has been able to grow its installed base around 18 percent per month on a global average.[14]

● *Early adopters*: Uber customers are often willing to pay premiums for what they consider to increase their individual welfare or improve their lifestyle. They also bet on the future lowering of prices of the innovation they are willing to adopt early. For example, the early adopters of smartphones were willing to pay a high price for their devices even if they assumed that with the development of technology and the widening of the markets prices would lower. Still, the gains of being an early adopter, of having direct and prime contact with the novelty and learning how to use it ahead of the masses as well as the exclusivity make it worthwhile paying the market premium. Marketing and early adopters have a symbiotic relationship. While marketing makes the novelty interesting for this group of consumers, they turn themselves into a vehicle of marketing in the diffusion of the novelty (Ferrell and Hartline 2012).

2.2.2   Uber Made a Difference

Explained as it was in the subsection above, Uber's business model does not seem out of the ordinary. But it made a difference because it was different and because it capitalized on this. Uber's business strategies mimic successful technology firms much more than transportation firms.[15] Uber saw a largely unperceived opportunity to revolutionize a technologically stagnant industry and uncovered a way of using innovation through technology to challenge the way the transportation industry works, which has left established firms vulnerable. 'Taxis, whose business model has hardly changed since the 1940s, have a lot to worry about. A taxicab company's technology and business model compare to Uber's like a Model T does to a Chevy Volt.'[16]

The critique of the taxicab sector has also been voiced several times and in several different settings: car transportation services worldwide are local industries with locally established firms that are heavily governed by local statutes. Firms in this transportation industry focus on the impact of government regulations and fuel surcharges. These firms yield returns that are regulated by the government, and as a result, there is very little incentive to invest in improving the riding experience. These companies do not invest in innovation as a priority and have assumed the industry will not change (see Bessant et al. 2006; Buckley 2015; Dempsey 1996 for the United States in general, Yang et al. 2002 for Hong Kong). See, for example, the average taxicab in London or New York City: only a minority has in-seat entertainment, only a minority is running on more energy efficiency (than regulations require), only a minority offer customer review, among other indicators (Nunes et al. 2013). Turning these criticisms into practice, Uber quickly exposed the vulnerability of this stagnant industry and produced a business strategy that appeals to new and existing customers of the incumbent firms.

Uber also differentiates itself in its relationship with its 'suppliers,' or the providers of free capacity. Uber's strategy is to set up these suppliers, and its drivers, with a lucrative revenue sharing contract. As mentioned earlier, the driver, or supplier of unused capacity, receives around 80 percent of the fare, Uber the other 20 percent, and, more importantly for Uber's success, it does not have to incur the expenses involved with car ownership, licenses, insurance, and day-to-day operational costs.[17] In order to guarantee quality, Uber has a driver monitoring program. Its users can see driver rankings and make decisions about different drivers for their commute. This ranking system motivates the drivers and sets high standards for the Uber experience. Drivers will be expected to be on time, have a clean car and offer professional services if they want to continue to be a part of this growing business model. And customers have access to this quality monitoring that is also a development tool.

Indubitably, Uber and other ride-sharing companies have brought a new element of competition to the taxi industry. One result has been a decline in the value of the limited issue taxi licenses that have traditionally restricted the number of authorized taxis in a given locale, as explained above. This, on its very own, impacted investors with stakes in taxi medallions, for example. Knock-on effects to the competition by ride-sharing companies include adverse changes to the financial position of lenders who have made taxi medallion loans that are too large a part of the total loan portfolio of the financial institution. Historically, some lenders have loaned up to 90 percent of a medallion's value. US companies like Signature Bank, Progressive Credit Union (85 percent of the total 625 million dollar loan portfolio was dedicated to taxi medallions in 2015) and Melrose Credit Union (which in 2015 had 2 billion dollars connected to taxi medallions) are all coming under solvency pressure. In addition, Citigroup has initiated foreclosure proceedings on 46 taxi medallions.[18]

A more systematic analysis of the differences between Uber and the 'traditional taxicab' industry can be made by comparing both, for example, using the following criteria (Perry 2015):[19]

- *Barriers to market entry*: while there are significant barriers to market entry in the traditional taxicab industry with medallions or licenses restricting competition, Uber poses none. Every person with a car and willing to enter a contractual relation can offer services.
- *Levels of service*: while traditional taxis must offer the one standard and regulated level, Uber has a variety of different service levels, for example, UberBLACK, UberSUV, UberX, UberPOP and so on. Granted, many of these were developed with time and some even in order to circumvent regulation. However, the diversity of service levels can only occur if a company is not regulated.
- *Pricing*: while taxicab prices are high and static, set or capped by regulation, Uber's pricing is generally lower and dynamic allowing for more influence by the market process. The cost for an average 5-mile trip for 21 major cities is 14.62 dollars plus tip for taxis and 11.20 dollars for Uber.
- *Tipping*: expected in traditional taxis and should amount to 10 to 20 percent of the ride price. For Uber, no tipping is expected.
- *Ease of payment*: while traditional taxicabs will mostly take cash and only some would accept credit cards, Uber only accepts credit cards.
- *Frequency of promotions and discounts*: traditional taxicabs cannot offer promotions or discounts, but Uber can and does.
- *Price estimation*: Uber provides customers with an estimated price before the ride, taxicabs do not.
- *Quality and cleanliness of vehicles*: taxicabs face regulation regarding these criteria, so they will opt for complying with the standards set by regulation. Uber drivers are evaluated by these criteria, so they have the incentive of offering above-average quality and cleanliness.
- *Professionalism of drivers*: taxi drivers are professionals; however, that does not mean that they are friendly. Uber drivers are rated, so they have an additional incentive for being friendlier. One could claim that taxi drivers have an incentive too, that is, the tip. However, at least in the United States, the tip is considered a fixed part of a price. Drivers expect the tip no matter what.

- *Driver feedback*: taxis have none, Uber has automated feedback.
- *Filing a complaint*: in Washington DC, for example, the procedure is time-consuming and resolution takes three days. Uber offers the possibility of rating the driver and even contacting him personally.
- The *consequences for drivers offering poor service* are almost none for taxicabs but the termination of their contract with Uber.
- Ability to *communicate with the driver* before and after the ride: Uber's clients can call or text the driver anytime, taxicab clients do not have this possibility.
- *Details of the ride* (knowing when the driver is going to arrive, his or her car, plate number): with taxicabs this is only possible for a very limited number of companies. In Uber, it is standard.
- *Business/corporate accounts*: only very few taxicab companies offer business accounts. And even then, they are just valid in the locale serviced by that specific company. Uber offers national and regional accounts.
- *Loyalty programs*: while traditional taxicabs only offer rudimentary loyalty programs, Uber introduced UberVIP, a program of its own.

2.2.3 Uber and Ethics

Apart from purely economic analyses of Uber, its business model, innovation and the role it plays, there are many other discussions about it happening, for example, if Uber's business model has ethical implications. While every business model has ethical implications, the question is better framed in terms of if there is anything specific in Uber's strategy that challenges ethical postulates. This is insinuated in questions such as: is Uber (and are other sharing economy companies) just exploring legal loopholes or is it setting up a legitimate business? Is Uber empowering the driver-partner or just creating more precarious freelancing jobs without security? Is Uber enhancing consumer experience or just using consumers as agents of quality control and a source of new data? Is Uber's pricing system fair revealing the scarcity of capacity or just an exploitation of the consumer's willingness to pay (surge pricing)? How can Uber, as a company that scarcely produces operative gains, have such a high stock valuation? In general, is it fair to unleash creative destruction?

Some of these questions echo the discussion about the sharing economy in Chapter 1. But specifically directed at Uber, one of the main issues is whether Uber is an inclusive business model or not. Inclusive means: does it bring more wage-earning opportunities to more people or is it just reducing the costs of employment? This is a debate that continues to play out across communities worldwide. While the conclusions are anything but clear, even as more data pour in, it is worth reviewing the available literature and knowing about the centers of the research debate and lines of argument. Hall and Kruger (2015) using Uber's internal data find clear benefits for driver-partners and note the new financial opportunities created for tens of thousands of workers. Those conclusions have been criticized by, for example, the liberal-leaning Center for Economic and Policy Research. In any case, Hall and Kruger's paper (2015, p. 14) also argues that the availability of modern technology, like the Uber app, provides many advantages and lowers prices for consumers compared with the traditional taxicab dispatch system, and this has boosted demand for ride services, which, in turn, has increased total demand for workers with the requisite skills to work as for-hire drivers, potentially raising earnings for all workers with such skills. Bernhardt (2014, p. 15) also signals a cautionary note about any claims of radical recent change being wrought across the US economy:

> We all share a strong intuition that the nature of work has fundamentally changed, contributing to the deterioration of labor standards. Yet at least with aggregate national data, it has been hard to find evidence of a strong, unambiguous shift toward nonstandard or contingent forms of work – especially in contrast to the dramatic increase in wage inequality. This is not to say that there have been no changes in the workplace. But as this paper has emphasized, for enforcement agencies and policymakers, it may be more fruitful to focus on specific industries and regions in assessing when and where pernicious forms of nonstandard work have grown, and which groups of workers have been most impacted.

A 2015 report from the Center for American Progress notes the heated debate in Britain over 'zero hours contracts' and charges that highly insecure and contingent employment leads to the exploitation of workers. The report notes that:

> Technology has allowed a sharing economy to develop in the United States; many of these jobs offer flexibility to workers, many of whom are working a second job and using it to build income or are parents looking for flexible work schedules. At the same time, when these jobs are the only source of income for workers and they provide no benefits, that leaves workers or the state to pay these costs. (Summers and Balls 2015, p. 32)

Meanwhile, scholars such as Schor (2014) and Benkler (2004) have been examining how workers or consumers might regain bargaining power through an increasingly app-based, decentralized system of distributed labor. 'While the for-profit companies may be "acting badly," these new technologies of peer-to-peer economic activity are potentially powerful tools for building a social movement centered on genuine practices of sharing and cooperation in the production and consumption of goods and services.' One might ask, then, how to achieve this. Schor (2014) has an answer: 'But achieving that potential will require democratizing the ownership and governance of the platforms.' For a more philosophical approach to the ethical conundrums imposed by the 'sharing economy,' refer to Ulrich (2008) and Stalder (2011). For one of the most complete accounts of the social and ethical issues that might be involved in Uber, refer to Rogers (2015).

However, even this discussion on the ethical implications of Uber's business model merits some critical assessment. Often, it is common to see 'job security,' 'wage fairness' and 'conditions of labor' as definable terms. Caution is needed. The content of all these expressions is (also) a result of subjective preferences and the circumstances in which they are used. Stipulating an *ex ante*, objective meaning of 'job security' or 'fair wage' is intellectually difficult because an account of what its respective elements are must be given. And any such account is subjected to Ockham's razor. In fact, the contemporary context shows that all these conceptions are malleable. The taxicab drivers' wage is fruit of negotiation and sometimes collective bargaining. Just the fact that this wage is open to bargaining shows that there is no objective measure for it.

There is even a more important question regarding most discussions of the ethics of Uber. As some of the passages quoted above show, it is assumed that companies exist in order to provide jobs. While many entrepreneurs do create jobs and even like doing so, why should that be an ethical obligation of a firm? The firm does not belong to its staff, or to its customers, but to the entrepreneur. From property follows responsibility. But what that responsibility entails can only be determined by the individual value – judgement of the entrepreneur. This does not amount to claiming that ethics itself is relative, but the ways of dealing with it, especially ethical dilemmas, are subjective. Instead, many self-styled inquiries over Uber's ethics often amount to calls for regulation disguised as philosophy.

With equal ethical conviction it can be claimed that Uber opens windows of entrepreneurial opportunity to many (drivers), increases the freedom of others (consumers) and even sets an example of how technology can be used in different parts of the economy. By being innovative, Uber is being ethical; this would be the other claim.

2.3   THE CASE OF UBER: UBERIZATION?

In the last section, Uber's startup business model was introduced and discussed in terms of its novelties and ethics. Uber's success can be measured in a different number of ways, one being if it inspired other entrepreneurs to follow the same path. The answer is yes. In fact, Uberization or Uberification are buzzwords coming out of Uber's success. And much like the 'sharing economy,' the discussion about this concept quickly runs to essentialisms. As done in Chapter 1 with the 'sharing economy,' this section tries to make sense of what might be referred to as 'Uberization.'

The idea behind Uberization is providing on-demand services for as many needs and preferences as possible. This idea is positioned so that for products and services that consumers would ordinarily have to engage in searching and evaluating, an app either discovers the service needed to fulfill the need in question or intermediates with a decentral supplier of the good that best matches the need. Boldly put, for every consumer demand, there will be a mobile app that can service that need.

By this logic, Uberization sees Uber not just as a taxi app, but as a blueprint for how to do 'convenience tech.' Uberization thinks that the real genius of Uber lies in a deep understanding of convenience – what it is and why it matters. The psychology of convenience that can be seen as the one common feature of Uberization comprises the following dimensions (Davis 2015):

1.   decision convenience – making it fast and easy to choose
2.   access convenience – making it fast and easy to acquire
3.   transaction convenience – making it fast and easy to pay
4.   benefit convenience – making it fast and easy to enjoy/use
5.   post-benefit convenience – making it fast and easy to re-purchase.

So why is Uber the role model for capitalizing on convenience? The simplest answer is that Uber promises to buy time and save effort. Customers have limited time and limited effort to give – and little preference to waste them on hailing taxicabs. In this way, by offering convenience, Uber becomes more attractive because it 'costs' less – not in money but in time and effort. By reducing time and effort costs, Uber delivers better value – without reducing the price. It understands that convenience is not just about saving physical effort and time but also saving mental time and effort. Some experiences are mentally inconvenient because they take mental time and effort to process emotionally and cognitively. Uber makes its taxi service emotionally convenient by giving passengers a good experience and rationale with a clear value promise that they will save precious time and effort. And this is the blueprint for Uberization.

On the other hand, are there certain contexts that lead to more or easier Uberization? Roughly, the following five conditions in the market processes favor capitalizing on convenience (Gapiński 2016). First, the individuals supplying the service are highly skilled, hard to find and specialized. When suppliers are hard to find, the transaction costs incurred in finding them can be extremely high – in comparison to the value of the good. The more highly skilled and specialized suppliers are, the harder to find they can be. If an intermediary is able to search and evaluate quickly and cheaply, this leads to more convenience. Referring to Uber, the question might arise as to how taxicab drivers can be described as highly skilled suppliers. The answer is that the high market entrance barriers make drivers (artificially) more difficult to find. Also, spending time searching for a taxicab is too costly in comparison to the utility of the good provided by the taxicab. In this sense, Uber's service perfectly fits the condition.

Second, unmet and growing demand in all segments of a business favors Uberization. In the taxicab industry, there was unmet demand because the supply was (artificially) capped by regulation. Also, different segments were prevented from emerging since regulation only foresees a very limited range of service levels. Uber matches 'excess demand' to other means of supply and expands the different segments of transportation. Uberization would apply this logic to other industries, for example, to eating, manufacturing or banking, again, if the intermediary is able to matchmake at low costs.

Third and narrowly related to the second, if there is no single supplier of any size presently able to meet the new demands, Uberization has a better chance of succeeding. This means finding and aggregating the different suppliers by this creating a scale each on its own cannot create. The perspective of creating economies of scale – diminishing average prices – is itself convenient because it usually demands intense investment.

The fourth and fifth conditions are similar. Little temporal flexibility and inelastic prices of demand (that is, demanded quantity is not sensitive to changes in price) contribute to Uberization. If a customer needs some service immediately, this customer will be willing to pay for inter-mediation or this customer will prefer the service that requires less time for search and assessment. The same applies to prices. If a customer does not care for lower prices, an intermediary that manages to sell conveni-ence profits from the customer's preparedness to pay high prices.

This section cannot discuss to the full extent what Uberization is. There are, as often, different conceptions of it. However, if Uberization is understood as capitalizing on convenience, it becomes clear that it is more than just a buzzword. It might even be the blueprint for innovating different sectors. If this blueprint works, however, depends on the conditions of different types of market processes. And of course it also depends on the entrepreneurship of market agents. Uber is an innovative company. That is beyond doubt. It changed many things in the taxicab industry. There is also little discussion about this. The question now is if Uber is really a disruptive innovator and an agent of creative destruction.

SUMMARY

What is Uber's business model? Uber capitalizes on convenience. In order to do so, it identifies idle capacity, aggregates it and allocates it to consumers willing to pay the price. Uber is an intermediary of idle capacity. This intermediation happens at lower costs, which allows Uber to create value-add to customers. It makes finding a taxicab easier, it provides different service levels, it gives information about the quality and price of the ride and it allows interaction. This value-add is redirected at the company in form of feedback by the customers prompting their trust and loyalty. Characterizing Uber as an intermediary, as a technology platform offering its services as a matchmaker for those willing to sell spare capacity of cars to those willing to pay for this capacity, is therefore correct. Uber could have applied this business model to other different sectors, but it chose transportation. Transportation, however, is not the core of what Uber is. Rather, it is just its application.

Answering the question about what Uber's business model is, is also answering the questions about what Uber is. And after arguing how Uber's business model can be expanded to other industries, Uberization, the next set of questions arises: Is Uber disruptive? Did it unleash creative destruction through disruptive innovation? What are the consequences of Uberization? These questions will be addressed in Chapter 3.

NOTES

1. Akerlof, however, can be criticized in a number of ways; for example, his framing of the problem is highly selective and biased. Even if there are no middlemen, market processes are always asymmetric in their information. The asymmetry is what drives people to the markets in the first place. Then, Akerlof has a biased view of the consumers, for he does

not allow them to gather information or, through cooperative practices, to mount pressure on vendors. Finally, his regulatory proposal is questionable. Regulation, too, is marked by asymmetries of information. Furthermore, there is little empirical evidence showing positive – or indeed any – results of regulating the dealers in information (Anderson 2001).

2. This was the absolutist monarch that fought first against Parliament and then against Oliver Cromwell (1599–1658). King Charles I (1600–1649) was found guilty of treason by a court of commoners and sentenced to death by decapitation. Under the administration of Cromwell, Lord Protector, and afterwards for-hire-coach-regulations and licenses continued.

3. One of Vienna's contemporary tourist attractions is rooted in this pre-regulatory past. As for-hire-coaches would assemble and wait for customers in front of the Parisian church of 'Saint Fiacre,' an innovative Viennese businessman just copied that concept in Vienna, letting coaches wait for customers in front of Vienna's cathedral, the Stephansdom. For marketing purposes and in order to show that these for-hire-vehicles were the latest fashion in France, he even used the French name of their stand: *Fiacre*. That is the origin of the popular Viennese *Fiaker*. This businessman, whose name is not known, was however more at ease than other hackney-coaches of his time: he also invented a licensing system to give him the monopoly over all *Fiaker* in Vienna (Barthel 1992).

4. Joseph Aloysius Hansom (1803–1882) was an English architect working principally in the Gothic Revival style.

5. This was the engineer Gottlieb Daimler (1834–1900) that patented the internal combustion engine and whose name later garnered the company's name Daimler-Benz – the manufacturer of Mercedes Benz.

6. Hearst (1863–1951) was himself a controversial figure. Politically standing on the left wing of the Progressive Movement, Hearst was also a politician. This Democrat then Independence Party figure served as Member of the US House of Representatives from New York's 11th district and ran unsuccessfully for Mayor of New York and Governor of New York. His newspapers took a fiercely pro-labor-movement stance and often engaged in yellow journalism – sensationalized stories featuring crime, corruption, sensation and sex, and of sometimes dubious veracity (Frazier 2001).

7. Washington Post (2012), 'Uber car impounded, driver ticketed in city sting,' accessed 20 May 2016 at https://www.washingtonpost.com/blogs/mike-debonis/post/uber-car-impounded-driver-ticketed-in-city-sting/2012/01/13/gIQA4Py3vP_blog.html.

8. Roadshow (2011), 'Uber lives on despite SFMTA cease-and-desist,' accessed 20 May 2016 at http://reviews.cnet.com/8301-13746_7-20025664-48.html.

9. Uber (2016), 'About,' accessed 20 May 2016 at https://www.uber.com/about.

10. Forbes (2014), 'A disruptive cab-ride to riches: the Uber payoff,' accessed 20 May 2016 at http://www.forbes.com/sites/aswathdamodaran/2014/06/10/a-disruptive-cab-ride-to-riches-the-uber-payoff/.

11. This and all information on pricing are in Uber (2015), 'Chicago prices,' accessed 20 May 2016 at https://www.uber.com/cities/chicago#cities.

12. A recent study for New York City has shown that this pricing model has remained stable. 'Uber appears more expensive for prices below 35 dollars and begins to become cheaper only after that threshold. As one would expect, the cheaper journeys are those that are in principle of shorter range. As observed in a variety of empirical data, human mobility tends to be characterized by a vast majority of short trips. This observation therefore suggests that Uber's economical model exploits this trend of human mobility in order to maximize revenue' (Salnikov et al. 2015, p. 2).

13. Bizjournal (2012), 'Rider seeking taxi-driver,' accessed 20 May 2016 at http://www.bizjournals.com/sanfrancisco/print-edition/2012/02/03/rider-seeking-taxi-driver.html.

14. GrowthHackers (2025), 'Uber,' accessed 20 May 2016 at https://growthhackers.com/companies/uber/.

15. See note 11.

16. Bacon, J. (2012), 'Innovation Uber alles,' accessed 20 May 2016 at http://www.washingtontimes.com/news/2012/feb/2/innovation-uber-alles.

17. CNN (2012), 'The trials of Uber,' accessed 20 May 2016 at http://tech.fortune.cnn.com/2012/02/02/the-trials-of-uber.
18. Ibid.
19. Note that being different or innovative in these criteria does not necessarily mean being better. What is normatively better can only be judged by individuals in the market processes. While Maria might enjoy using a credit card, Joe still wants to pay cash. The criterion for differentiation or innovation allows companies and individuals to test other ways of behaving in the market processes.

3. What are creative destruction and disruption innovation?

For a long time, creative destruction remained an obscure term coined by an even more obscure economist. Then it became the buzzword of the so-called new economy. These were the high-growth industries on the cutting edge of technology and a driving force of economic growth. The new economy is commonly believed to have started in the late 1990s, as high-tech tools, such as the internet, and increasingly powerful computers began penetrating the consumer and business marketplace (Laffey 2006).

Creative destruction is still used in tech-savvy sectors and by many analysts trying to capture a simple idea: innovation transforms the economy and society. For many economists, however, this intuition is not enough, for they often need a more specific theory. One that identifies the elements of creative destruction and at least hints at how certain outcomes can be predicted. The mainstream economy has trouble with the concept of creative destruction because it explains things after they happened and does not offer an analytic way of anticipating them. For this type of economics, creative destruction is little more than a useful metaphor. From the point of view of Austrian economics, there is more about it than meets the eye. And at the same time, there is less.

In this chapter, two explanations of what creative destruction is will be reviewed. The first one is the economist Schumpeter's and the second, more modern, the management theorist Christensen's. Although they are in many ways similar, they are not identical. Christensen's theory has a more analytical background and more inductive power on the microeconomic level. But Schumpeter's idea is backed by strong intuition and allows for a macroeconomic perspective. In this sense, they complement each other. Reconnecting some of the preliminary thoughts explained in Chapter 1, this chapter will use the conception of markets as undetermined, dynamic, open-ended processes for understanding creative destruction and disruptive innovation.

Much has been written about these two concepts and their respective authors. This chapter, however, goes back to their texts and familiarizes readers with the authors themselves, rather than with secondary literature about them. The chapter is structured in the same way as the last two. After developing a theoretical framework, its application to the case study of the book follows. While the first and second sections of this chapter are dedicated to the theories of creative destruction and disruptive innovation, the third is their application to the case of Uber.

3.1 SCHUMPETER'S CREATIVE DESTRUCTION

Creative destruction is a rather complicated idea with a simple intuition at its core. It comes up in the work of an economist deeply preoccupied with the future of economics and capitalism. It also does not arise as a stand-alone idea but as one of several other forces that this economist explores. It is therefore important to know which place within the work of Schumpeter creative destruction has in order to fully understand it. That is why this section first reviews the context of the idea and then goes deeper into it.

3.1.1　Cycles and Fears

It was the Austrian-American economist Joseph Schumpeter who coined the term creative destruction as a shorthand description of the free market's anarchical (open-ended, without end-states, optima or equilibria) way of developing. In *Capitalism, Socialism, and Democracy* (1942, p. 83), he writes:

> The opening up of new markets, foreign or domestic, and the organizational development from the craft shop to such concerns as U.S. Steel illustrate the same process of industrial mutation – if I may use that biological term – that incessantly revolutionizes the economic structure from within, incessantly destroying the old one, incessantly creating a new one. This process of creative destruction is the essential fact about capitalism.

Schumpeter does not develop a full economic theory of creative destruction. Indeed, he only devotes a mere six-page chapter to 'The process of creative destruction' in which he describes capitalism as 'the perennial gale of creative destruction' (1942, p. 84). In the text, Schumpeter uses that expression rather vaguely, or as a metaphor for a process or a series of processes that sometimes revolutionize the economy. As an economist loosely[1] persuaded by the Austrian School in Economics, Schumpeter might not have intended to develop any prescriptive theory after all. More likely is his descriptive intention. After having analysed business and economic cycles, Schumpeter is interested in how these relate to more fundamental questions like democracy or the future of capitalism, for example, This relationship, Schumpeter finds, is contingent on several factors. It cannot be foreseen or predicted, it only can be described.

The Austrian School tends to acknowledge that there is always more to the market processes than individual theories can understand, predict or let alone prescribe. This can be either because markets are a very extensive organizational principle or because market processes are the potentially infinite sum of all its agents and the probabilities[2] of their exchanges. These market processes are chaotic by nature because the agents engaging in them are free and act freely. In particular, the agents judge outcomes as a function of their subjective preferences. As such, if market processes generate any order, then it is spontaneous order. Such order cannot be known or predicted in advance. But it can be explained and its influencing factors analysed.

This dynamic understanding of market processes advanced in Chapter 1 entails that no single person or body of people knows more about the market than the market itself does, and even 'the market' knows nothing: Since markets are nothing more than a series of revealed preferences and individual exchanges between market agents, there is nothing to know apart from the information stock they reveal. The claim to know more than the markets entails knowing about each individual's set of preferences including their dynamics. This is a very ambitious claim – at least. Markets themselves cannot have an epistemic state because they don't exist as a separate entity, but as processes. It follows from this that it is extremely difficult, if not impossible, to find general (scientific) patterns about how markets behave. And then, if it is not possible to formulate general patterns, it is not possible to develop general prescriptions (or regulations).

Caution is required when ascribing all of these views in this precise way to Schumpeter. In his early work, *Theory of Economic Development* (1911), he seems to advocate or at least accept and search for general patterns (or covering laws) in economics. Also, in *Business Cycles* (1939), Schumpeter is still searching for overarching economics patterns, however, as he explains, only in a descriptive manner (1939, p. vi). In those two books, Schumpeter writes about the economic cycle and its constants, its dependence on exogenous factors, economic development and so on. However, he also claims that the spontaneity of entrepreneurship is central to the markets. And as this spontaneity is difficult to foresee, it is difficult to predict the calculations and miscalculations of the individual agents. At the end, Schumpeter sees not general equilibria but phases of growth and crisis, or boom-and-bust cycles. In his conclusion, these cycles are not only the rule in economic development but also necessary to it – caution: necessary does not mean predictable. After all, no one is well informed all of the time. No one knows the ideal amount of investment all the time and no one has strategies with guaranteed success. Even after having arrived at this open-textured conclusion, Schumpeter remains modest about its generalization. In his view, his theory is a descriptive device, but a device that cannot describe the whole of the market reality; just parts of it (McCraw 2006).

In *Capitalism, Socialism, and Democracy* (1942), Schumpeter changes his mind about the nature of markets once again. He loses his interest in 'the market' and directs his attention to its agents; in this case, to entrepreneurs, the challenges they face and the challenges that arise from their activities. It is in this book that creative destruction is formally introduced. It is of course difficult to say why he does not expand on it. But there might be three reasons.

First, if the market is nothing more than the sum of the individuals and groups of individuals as well as their potentially infinite possibilities of exchange, it is extremely difficult to assess which drivers, processes and outcomes markets have and will have. Second, if creative destruction exists, it must be fuzzy by nature. Finding law-like content in it is anathema to the theory itself. Third, and most likely, Schumpeter is not interested in developing a theory per se, because he is more concerned with the possible outcomes of creative destruction. His book is written during World War II. With the rise of national socialism, socialism and Keynesianism, Schumpeter not only changes his opinion about the nature of markets, he also changes his mind on the outcomes of capitalism. Schumpeter fears that capitalism would not survive itself. Most Austrian economists of his time thought that defending free markets against collectivist theories was the way to go. Schumpeter, who endorsed free markets, asks if there is something in the market processes that might destroy them from within. Creative destruction bears this potential in his opinion. It's a source of good and evil, in his judgement.

Some caveats are warranted here. It is doubtful whether Schumpeter has any fully developed theory of what creative destruction is, how it works and what outcomes it produces. It is more realistic to think of him as answering to Marx's different claims of class struggle, system destruction and new beginning (Elliott 1980). Some interpretations go so far as to state that Schumpeter believes in the destruction of capitalism itself – as a system – through creative destruction, and not through class struggle (Müller 1983). It is true: sometimes, Schumpeter feels deeply skeptical of the capitalistic system as a whole, either thinking that only the large and wealthy conglomerates that can fund innovation would survive, or even implying that capitalism has no future. It is in the preface of the same book that Schumpeter states: 'I felt it my duty to take, and to inflict upon the reader, considerable trouble in order to lead up effectively to my paradoxical conclusion: capitalism is being killed by its achievements' (1942, p. xiv). And cut to the chase with: 'The capitalist process shapes things and souls for socialism' (1942, p. 220).

This interpretation, however, misses his point because it does not differentiate between what Schumpeter factually studies and what his normative preferences and fears are. Granted, he himself very often does not differentiate between factual and normative statements. But even on a normative level, Schumpeter remained 'agnostic' in the sense of indecisive about the future of capitalism and even about how to repair it – if any repairs were needed. In this last stage of his work, Schumpeter is radically anti-prescriptive. Some would also claim he is radically pessimistic.

How then to read him claiming that creative destruction leads capitalism to socialism? First, Schumpeter does not claim that creative destruction inevitably leads to the destruction of capitalism. He states, however, that there is a possibility that it would. For no one knows the future. Schumpeter endorses capitalism as a normative desideratum; however, he is wary of his times' problems. He sees the rise of Marxism-Leninism and Nazi Germany as real threats and he understands the ideas of Keynes as a serious challenge of capitalism from within. On this normative level, Schumpeter is afraid that it would be impossible for capitalism to persist, simply because the world is not letting it continue. 'Capitalism stands its trial before judges who have the sentence of death in their pockets. They are going to pass it, whatever the defense they may hear; the only success victorious defense can possibly produce is a change in the indictment' (1942, p. 144).

It is the general pessimism of his time that makes him stress the negative potential of creative destruction. But there is a creative potential too. And this creative potential is at the root of Schumpeter's thought: entrepreneurs discover novelties and market them. This is the analytical core of creative destruction – and this core is very different from the fears of its outcomes at the macroeconomic and political levels.

3.1.2 Entrepreneurship and Destruction

Creative destruction, as the name reveals, has a creative core. It is the entrepreneur seizing an opportunity and introducing something new to the market processes. Schumpeter is very flexible in his definition of novelty, for he accepts some new technology, but also new ways of organizing work, new services and even marketing as a novelty. Sometimes, even relaunching or rebranding traditional goods might qualify as a novelty. For Schumpeter, there is no way of identifying what the market processes will accept as a novelty. Also, there is no way of anticipating how this novelty is going to impact or change the market processes. It is the entrepreneur that discovers the novelty and if this novelty is accepted as such by the market processes through its immersion in these processes. Not every innovation automatically leads to creative destruction. Creative destruction occurs when a novelty radically changes all competitors and the way the agents in the market processes behave in these processes. After creative destruction has occurred, there is no fallback into the character of the market processes as it was before creative destruction. This also entails that if and how a novelty unleashed creative destruction can only be analysed after it happened. This flexibility in the description of elements and outcomes of creative destruction is an open-textured definition. It is open for its explicative power might be high, but its predictive and prescriptive powers are low.

Schumpeter's language often does not differentiate between the single capitalist and the capitalistic system as a whole. Indeed, when introducing the entrepreneurship behind creative destruction, he cares a lot less about the system per se than he does about individual firms and their actions, especially innovation. That is why the analytical side of Schumpeter's approach can best be understood as an inquiry into entrepreneurialism. The overarching systems of socialism, capitalism and democracy are analysed in terms of how entrepreneurialism impacts on them and how they are impacted by entrepreneurialism. And within this approach to entrepreneurialism it is a fact that companies 'destroy' each other. 'Destruction' means companies challenge each other through innovation; the continuous series of challenges can even drive companies or whole business models out of the market. Destruction, understood this way, has a much less negative connotation than it generally has. Indeed, each entrepreneur anticipates his own destruction as early as becoming an entrepreneur.

In the paragraph above and for Schumpeter himself, there is no mention of the 'survival of the fittest.' But often that image is conjured when creative destruction is discussed. In economics there is even a subdiscipline called 'evolutionary economics' that often takes Darwinian views. Schumpeter, however, does not belong to that line of thought. The term was coined by Thorstein Veblen (1857–1929), an American economist and sociologist.[3] Veblen's evolutionary economics drew upon anthropology, sociology, psychology and explicitly Darwinian principles (further examples of social Darwinism are in biology (Paul 1988) and in social sciences (Bouchard 2011)). Evolutionary economists believe that economic organization is a dynamic process involving ongoing trans-formation, and that economic behavior is determined by both individuals and society as a whole. There are readings of Schumpeter in light of social Darwinism, the theory that persons, groups and races are subject to the same laws of natural selection as Charles Darwin had perceived in plants and animals in nature (Dickens 2000, p. 16), and evolutionary economics. A good example of this is Kelm's (1997) 'Schumpeter's theory of economic evolution: a Darwinian interpretation.'

Hodgson (1997) replies to Kelm's (1997, p. 98) claim stating that Schumpeter is evolutionary, but not in a Darwinian sense. 'The essential point to grasp is that in dealing with capitalism we are dealing with an evolutionary process' (Schumpeter 1942, p. 82). The ideas of survival and fitness are even used by Schumpeter, but the process that he has in mind is not determined by any antecedent facts such as genetic material and the like, let alone by covering laws of nature. The process of evolution shows the same open texture that marks the definition of creative destruction. In Schumpeter's meaning, evolution is a series of open-ended, undetermined processes. It is neither causally dependent on its outputs nor on its organization. This moment of continuous non-teleological, non-causal change as one essence of the capitalist system is central to *Capitalism, Socialism, and Democracy*. Schumpeter states:

> As a matter of fact, capitalist economy is not and cannot be stationary. Nor is it merely expanding in a steady manner. It is incessantly being revolutionized from within by new enterprise, i.e., by the intrusion of new commodities or new methods of production or new commercial opportunities into the indus-trial structure as it exists at any moment. (1942, p. 31)

For Schumpeter, evolution in economics is nothing more than the continuous process of innovation by entrepreneurs and reaction to innovation by the other agents in the market processes, especially by other entrepreneurs. And innovation is by definition a non-deterministic, non-foreseeable, non-causal, non-teleological process. Therefore, Schum-peter only shows linguistic proximity to evolutionary economics. He is radically anti-causal and anti-deterministic. Only time and the develop-ment of the market processes will tell and show what human society accepts as innovation and what propels evolution.

This also explains why Schumpeter does not develop an analytical account of what creative destruction is. It can take so many different forms that there is little gain in explaining any one of them. It is Clayton Chistensen that attempts to give a more fine-grained and functional answer to the question of how creative destruction works. His answer is: creative destruction works through disruptive innovation. But before disruptive innovation is discussed, let Schumpeter's train of thought be finished.

Schumpeter is interested in how other entrepreneurs – and society – act and react in relation to creative destruction. As a process, it has no defined end-state, but offers many different possible outcomes. Some of these outcomes and impacts benefit and some are detrimental to society, as he perceived it. This also explains why Schumpeter does not use the figure of speech of creative destruction to legitimize innovation. He does not say that any innovation or creative destruction can be counter-balanced or dealt with by the other agents of the market processes. In fact, analytically Schumpeter remains largely agnostic about the desirability of the effects of creative destruction. He wants to look at them, but he does not want to judge them.

It is this inner duality of creative destruction that Schumpeter was trying to express: the process often does destroy actual structures. And destruction comes at a cost. Business models fail, people lose jobs and capital gains disappear. He claims: 'Situations emerge in the process of creative destruction in which many firms may have to perish that nevertheless would be able to live on vigorously and usefully if they could weather a particular storm' (1942, p. 90). In the center of creative destruction are creativity, innovation and the ability to market new products. These factors themselves are not for free either. Since innovation is not a process with determinate or determinable outputs, engaging in creative behavior and marketing new ideas involves incurring risks, and thus involves multiple failures. All these conditions need capital and knowledge in order to start and be maintained. In other words, in order to innovate, the entrepreneur needs money and knowledge. And the entrepreneur can only have access to both if success has already materialized. The cell phone producer Nokia is an example. It accumulated capital selling galoshes. It invested this capital in the development of technology and it became a cell phone producer. With time, the business unit in charge of the galoshes was closed. Through capital and knowledge, creativity and innovation build upon the very basis they could destroy. And this is an important lesson for the driver of destruction as well; once it has destroyed past products, services and business models, it inherently becomes the object of possible further destruction. 'Any existing structures and all the conditions of doing business are always in a process of change. Every situation is being upset before it has had time to work itself out. Economic progress, in a capitalist society, means turmoil' (1942, p. 51). Because of the costs of innovation and the absorption of these costs as well as the results of the process themselves (the destruction of parts of the very business model), Schumpeter thinks that only large corporations could afford innovation. And here again, his pessimism resurfaces: 'For one thing, to predict the advent of big business was considering the conditions of Marx's day an achievement in itself' (1942, p. 34).

There are two more observations about Schumpeter's creative destruction to make before continuing. The first refers to the relationship of invention, innovation and technology. And the second is about the role of the working class.

First, innovation should not necessarily be thought of as a technological advancement. Often, innovation is just an idea or even the return of an old idea in a new framework. Sears was not driven out of business by the internet but by companies like Wal-Mart (value proposition: cheap) or GAP (value proposition: quality) (Rugman and Girod 2003). Or take, for example, the rise of vintage or retro products. They exemplify that innovation is not always about new technology. By the way, invention does not equal innovation, for the innovative entrepreneur can introduce the invention or the idea in the market, hence the importance of marketing. In the *Theory of Economic Development* (1911, p. 109) Schumpeter makes it clear that 'Innovation is the market introduction of a technical or organizational novelty, not just its invention.'

Second, Schumpeter is also very preoccupied with the effects of creative destruction on the labor markets. He recognizes that the paradox of creative destruction not only has an effect on the companies and on society as a whole but also on the supply side of labor, on the employed and unemployed personally. A society cannot reap the rewards of creative destruction without accepting that some individual agents might be worse off, not just in the short term but perhaps forever. At the same time, attempts to soften the harsher aspects of creative destruction by trying to preserve jobs or protect industries will lead to stagnation. Schumpeter's enduring term reminds us that capitalism's pain and gain are inextricably linked. The process of creating new industries cannot go forward without sweeping away the preexisting order. Technology roils job markets, as Schumpeter conveys in coining the phrase 'technological unemployment.' However, he is also persuaded by the idea that over time – a time that could be longer than an individual's time span – the supply side of labor markets would adjust (1942, p. 35).

Does that mean that Schumpeter is an anti-capitalist and that creative destruction is, after all, leading society to turmoil and socialism? No. Schumpeter believes that creative destruction might pose social problems. But he also thinks that only individuals can judge how desirable certain outcomes are. While he accepts that creative destruction often produces desirable outcomes, he also says that it is not necessarily so. If endorsers of capitalism claim that its forces, including creative destruction, actually helped or advanced society at large and could or will continue to do so, then this is a claim based on the empirical results of capitalism in the last century and not a Schumpeterian claim that creative destruction always brings gains in the long run. Of course, in its aftermath, capitalism brought many individuals and countries much advancement, for example, increase in individual wealth, more and better education, better health and so on (see, for example, Frieden and Kennedy 2006; Seldon 2004). But these are the contingent results of the open-textured process and there is no guarantee that these results will always be achieved.

Where does this leave us? For Schumpeter, the process of creative destruction is fundamentally open, non-deterministic and non-teleological. This means that no agent knows the outcomes of that process and the process itself is not determined by its inputs. It is imaginable that creative destruction, in the end, will destroy the creator himself (think of Atari and video games). It is equally imaginable that creative destruction will lead to monopolies (as in the case of Microsoft). And it is also possibly the case that creative destruction can lead to more competition or even freer markets. This is the case of photography, where the duopoly of Kodak and Fuji has been broken by different technologies and ultimately by the smartphone allowing everyone to take as many pictures as possible. Another case of creative destruction leading to more competition and freer markets is the possibility of buying books, apparel and even household appliances on the internet. Yet another case is web-based financial services: individual investors can trade in the stock market without the need of an intermediary. Creative destruction is a fundamentally entrepreneurial activity. It is the art of taking advantage of a moment. However, for Schumpeter, this entrepreneurialism is not only dependent on the capabilities and willingness of agents in market processes but also on their financial means. So, at the same time, creative destruction is open to all and limited to some. In 1911, Schumpeter stated:

> Only a few people possess the quality of leadership the quality of actually introducing and undertaking new combinations which is quite a different thing from inventing them. However, if one or a few have advanced with success, many of the difficulties disappear. Others can then follow these pioneers, as they will clearly do under the stimulus of the success now obtainable. Their success again makes it easier … for more people to follow suit, until finally the innovation becomes familiar and the acceptance of it a matter of free choice … The successful appearance of an entrepreneur (one

who carries out new combinations) is followed by the appearance, not simply of some others, but of ever greater numbers, though progressively less qualified ... Every normal boom starts in one or a few branches of industry and ... derives its character from the innovations in the industry where it begins. But the pioneers remove the obstacles for the others, not only in the branch of production in which they first appear, but, owing to the nature of these obstacles, ipso facto in other branches too. (p. 235)

3.2 CHRISTENSEN'S DISRUPTIVE INNOVATION

Schumpeter's theory can come as a 'cold shower.' He gives particular emphasis to the open texture of creative destruction. Speaking about creative destruction in the context of the new economy has little to do with the meaning of the term 'creative destruction' in Schumpeter's work. In fact, he often expresses pessimism. He also remains opaque about what precisely is attributing creative destruction to entrepreneurialism. Clayton Christensen, on the other hand, not only wants to find out how creative destruction works but is interested in telling companies and managers what they can do in order to trigger and manage it. In a later stage of his research, he also wants to be able to foresee which types of innovation can destroy or disrupt the market processes. This section first explains Christensen's approach and then merges both ideas into one model.

3.2.1 Using Disruptiveness

What is the operative driver of creative destruction? Disruptive innovation is the probabilistic mechanism behind creative destruction. Creative destruction describes the potential impact of innovation. Disruptive innovation is its inner development. Disruptive innovation describes a process by which a product or service takes root initially in simple applications at the bottom of a market and then relentlessly moves up the market, eventually displacing established competitors. Christensen extensively explored the concept in the 1990s, and presented it in his 1997 book *The Innovator's Dilemma* and has expanded it ever since. Christensen defines a disruptive innovation as a product or service designed for a new set of customers:

Generally, disruptive innovations were technologically straightforward, consisting of off-the-shelf components put together in a product architecture that was often simpler than prior approaches. They offered less of what customers in established markets wanted and so could rarely be initially employed there.

> They offered a different package of attributes valued only in emerging markets remote from, and unimportant to, the mainstream. (1997, p. 15)

Christensen argues that disruptive innovations can hurt successful, well-managed companies that are responsive to their customers and have excellent research and development. These companies tend to ignore the markets most susceptible to disruptive innovations because these bottom markets have very tight profit margins and are too small to provide a good growth rate to an established (sizable) firm. Thus, disruptive technology provides an example of when the common business world advice to 'focus on the customer' can sometimes be strategically counterproductive.

Christensen distinguishes between 'low-end disruption' that targets customers who do not need the full performance valued by customers at the high end of the market and 'new-market disruption' that targets customers who have needs that were previously unserved by existing incumbents (1997, p. 23).

'Low-end disruption' occurs when the rate at which products improve exceeds the rate at which customers can adopt the new performance. Therefore, at some point the performance of the product overshoots the needs of certain customer segments. At this point, a disruptive technology may enter the market and provide a product that has lower performance than the incumbent but which exceeds the requirements of certain segments, thereby gaining a foothold in the market.

> Disruption often paralyzes industry-leading companies, which are more accustomed to bringing about sustaining innovations. In other words, established companies are motivated to focus on pushing innovations to meet the needs of their high-end customers (it's hard to turn away from your most profitable customers). This leaves the door open for new entrants to target your low-end customers. Eventually, however, the new entrant will make improvements and move up-market – now targeting your high-end customers. (Christensen 1997, p. 29)

In low-end disruption, the disruptor is focused initially on serving the least profitable customer, who is happy with a good enough product. This type of customer is not willing to pay a premium for enhancements in product functionality. Once the disruptor has gained a foothold in this customer segment, it seeks to improve its profit margin. To get higher profit margins, the disruptor needs to enter the segment where the customer is willing to pay a little more for higher quality. To ensure this quality in its product, the disruptor needs to innovate. The incumbent will not do much to retain its share in a not so profitable segment, and will move up-market and focus on its more attractive customers. After a number of such encounters, the incumbent is squeezed into smaller markets than it was previously serving. And then finally the disruptive technology meets the demands of the most profitable segment and drives the established company out of the market. 'New-market disruption' occurs when a product fits a new or emerging market segment that is not being served by existing incumbents in the industry.

Some examples might put this into perspective: the Sony Walkman destroyed the idea of music as something that can only be enjoyed statically. Yes, the quality of music was at the beginning often bad; but it soon caught up. The iPod destroyed the Sony Walkman as the idea of having a limited amount of music on the go. The iPhone destroyed the iPod and the idea of multiple devices per person. Destruction in the Schumpeterian sense does not occur by products but by the ideas behind the products. If these ideas meet technology that makes them real, they are the disruptive innovation of which Christensen speaks. These ideas are shaped by predecessor ideas, and they themselves advance those ideas that bear the potential for their own destruction, or: going from the iPod to the iPhone is just following the logic of mobility. This is an example in 'new-market disruption.'

Other examples of disruptive innovation are: the personal computers that destroyed mainframe computers and are being destroyed by laptop computers (new market); the internet provides the disruptive technology that shops like Amazon need to destroy the business models of traditional full-service department stores (low end) and these stores themselves are destroying their traditional business through innovative marketing selling a lifestyle instead of products (new market); cellular phones are the disrupting innovation behind the destruction of fixed line telephony (what began as a new market is now also a low-end disruption); and retail medical clinics are destroying the traditional doctor's offices through disruptive innovations such as leaner processes, economies of scale and more affordable technology (low end) (Christensen et al. 2015).

Disruptive innovation is the continued movement of, metaphorically speaking, a force through a (non-deterministic) chain, or, less meta-phorically, the continuous development of technology that pushes the operationalization of an idea and its logical derivatives. The input is disruptive innovation and the outcome is the process of creative destruction.

A direct comparison of Christensen and Schumpeter warrants some caveats. While Schumpeter had a very broad understanding of what innovation can be, Christensen is more focused on technology. At least, he understands technology as the main facilitator of innovation and disruption. He presupposes that technology can lower the prices of products, thus making it easier to introduce them at the low end. Schumpeter accepts marketing, the organization of a firm, the organization of production, the legal form of the firm and so on as forms of innovation equal to technology. Although this is not contrary to Christensen, his paradigmatic case of innovation is technology.

Then, and on a more philosophical level, Christensen is Austrian inspired but not an Austrian economist in the strict sense. Quite the contrary: he is not overly interested in the general consequences of disruptive innovation for the economy or society nor does he engage in questions concerning the economic theory behind creative destruction. He is interested in the input of creative destruction – disruptive innovation – in order to make it adaptable and manageable. While Schumpeter wants to understand creative destruction, Christensen is about using disruptive innovation. No wonder why: as a management theorist, Christensen is about to develop management tools. These tools might share some descriptive intention with Schumpeter's theory, but their purpose is a normative one (Christensen 2006). This means that Christensen's aim is to offer practical advice for companies in becoming the disruptive innovator or successfully reacting to it. This becomes apparent when he claims: 'One secret to maintaining a thriving business is recognizing when it needs a fundamental change' (Christensen et al. 2008, p. 57), or in one of his newest books (Christensen et al. 2013), in which he develops five skills of the disruptive innovator: associating, questioning, observing, networking and experimenting.

But even if Christensen's theory is a normative one, it does not follow that it claims epistemic privilege over market process nor that it can be used as a prognostic one (in the macroeconomic sense of prognosis). What Christensen intends is to provide tools for using and navigating disruptive innovation. Using these tools does not guarantee an outcome. It makes innovation more manageable and therefore increases the likelihood of success. Ultimately, success is still dependent on the entrepreneurialism of those using the tools, on their means and on the reactions by other agents in the market processes. And all of these remain uncertain. Therefore, Christensen's approach, too, cannot be used for judging, justifying or regulating outcomes.

Keeping in mind that Schumpeter's is a descriptive theory in economics and Christensen's a normative approach for businesses, the next question arises: Who can become an agent of creative destruction through disruptive innovation?

Schumpeter very likely thinks that conglomerates and large enterprises have an advantage over small- and medium-sized ones, or even over startups, because they can better absorb the risks of ventures, they have larger budgets for innovation and they can control the timing of innovation according to their own product life cycle. In Schumpeter's defense, in his time, education was significantly less widespread in society than it is today, and the industrial means of production to which he refers were much more concentrated, as were financial capabilities. Also, the emergence of effects of scale and the introduction of industrial organization[4] seemed to push production economics toward large conglomerates (McCraw 2006, p. 241). Here, Christensen offers the better, more open explanation: ideas can come from everywhere, and just as larger entities can better influence the flow of ideas through their structure, it is the same structure that can slow down ideas and make one's own products vulnerable to innovation coming from outside the company. Presently, even the smallest entities with good ideas can launch them, thus becoming agents of creative destruction. There is a large enough stock of human capital both inside and outside all enterprises. Ironically, Schumpeter himself recognized this: 'it is leadership rather than ownership that matters' (1939, p. 103).

Thinking of some of the examples of Chapter 2, it wasn't always the large corporation with an overflow of financial means that innovated. Allen's, as he brought the taxicab to New York City, was a small enterprise. He succeeded in obtaining means even without a corporate body behind him. What happened was his firm grew. The same can be said for Hertz or the architect Hansom. These were all small entrepreneurs that challenged the market processes through innovation. Since their innovation also destroyed the other agents, they grew to become the strongest agent in the market processes. But eventually, they too were destroyed – Hertz even destroyed himself.

This multi-sided feature of innovation is better grasped by Christensen. His idea of technology-backed disruption explains well how a one-man show such as architect Hansom can revolutionize the whole hackney cab industry. He comes up with a smaller, faster, cheaper model. The same applies to Allen. He comes up with a motor vehicle and a taximeter. Note, however, how Christensen's theory lacks an account for important aspects of some business models. Disruptive innovation would play the role of marketing down. But it was Allen's yellow cab that grabbed people's attention. Even Uber, with all its technology, follows a strategy in which marketing plays a crucial rule. Innovation is not about invention alone, it is also about marketing the products of invention. This does not mean Christensen does not care for these factors. He does, for example, when saying:

The technological changes that damage established companies are usually not radically new or difficult from a technological point of view. They do, however, have two important characteristics: First, they typically present a different package of performance attributes – ones that, at least at the outset, are not valued by existing customers. Second, the performance attributes that existing customers do value improve at such a rapid rate that the new technology can later invade those established markets. (Christensen 1995, p. 3)

Even if the demand side of the market processes do not seem to be the drivers of disruptive innovation, they are essential to the process nevertheless. It is the innovator who has to find out what the other agents want. To know the opportunity to seize is part of the innovator's entrepreneurship. And to know how to sell this innovation or address the agents in the market is part of that entrepreneurship too. In Christensen's theory, technological innovation is the necessary condition for disruption. But a company only becomes a true disruptive innovator if it knows how to address the other agents in the market processes. So, strategy, business plans, marketing and organization are the sufficient conditions for disruptive innovation.

There is a great deal of criticism toward Christensen's disruptive innovation. Jill Lepore, a Harvard-based management theorist, criticizes him heavily in a *New Yorker* article (2014). Among other things, she voices concern over what she perceives to be Christensen's bias in collecting data, his arbitrariness in explaining and assessing success and his inflationary use of the term innovation. Lepore might not be wrong, but she is not right. Her problem is demanding too much from Christensen's theory. That might be propelled by Christensen himself demanding too much of it. But what is it that Lepore misunderstands about Christensen? Disruptive innovation cannot explain every type of innovation. It is especially useful to describe technology-backed innovation. Also, it is not meant to have any general prognostic power; it increases the probability of success, but it cannot guarantee it. Christensen's theory is a utilitarian tool and not a scientific model. This does not in any case diminish its merits; if anything, it increases them – and makes it better understandable.

3.2.2 Making Sense of it All

Creative destruction and disruptive innovation complement each other. But this is not immediately apparent, for there are considerable differences. To what extent they complement each other has to be explained. Christensen's disruptive innovation provides an insight into the input of

the process. Creative destruction is about the inventiveness of entrepreneurship and putting its outcome in an overall context. Both theories
represent trade-offs.

Schumpeter is a good beginning for showing this trade-off (and also to
what degree he still thought in 'classic' economic terms). Schumpeter
thinks that the demand side of the market is a given; there is not more
demand in function of a new or better product. Innovation-at-large
creates costs. In a dynamic process, some of these costs can be passed on
to the demand side through a higher price. But as companies do this, the
higher price decreases the demanded quantity of a good. In this view,
which does not allow for the expansion of demand and the market itself,
selling a lesser quantity of new products at a higher price does not lead to
a process in which demanders adopt this new product. The alternative is
not to pass on these costs. That means that the innovator would have to
absorb all the costs of innovating. If the innovator absorbs the costs of
innovation, it can still sell the demanded quality of the goods at the price
demand is used to – but of the new good. This explains why in
Schumpeter's view only large conglomerates would be able to afford
innovation. However, in reality the demand side is not a given. In a
market process view, demand is as flexible as supply and is itself
influenced by innovation and its marketing. With the development of new
products, the demanded quantity expands because of the additional
agents that decide to consume the novelty. Sometimes, these are even
willing to pay higher prices, because they are a new type of customer.
(First-mover customers were happy to pay more for the first gramophone
as well as happy to pay the high prices of an iPhone.) Furthermore,
innovation also triggers the interest of investors.

If Schumpeter then misses this, how can it be corrected? Taking supply
and demand as static elements of the market is the most important
miscalculation in Schumpeter's idea, for the trade-off is not one of supply
and demand but in the analysis of expected cost-benefit from the
perspective of the individual innovator. This trade-off encompasses two
sides. On the one side, there are the expected costs of innovation-at-large.
On the other side, there are the expected benefits of innovating. While the
costs occur at the level of a company, it is the society of agents that
freely participate in the market processes that benefits from innovation.
The innovator has no immediate return; the best it can expect is a
winner-takes-all outcome. This asymmetry escapes Schumpeter. Christensen is more attuned to it as he distinguishes between the innovation as
such and the effort of introducing it. An innovator must persevere for a
long time until its novelties have a foothold in the market processes and
start disrupting them. If an innovation is truly disruptive, it affects all

agents on the supply side. More precisely, it will drive (most of) them out of the market. This means, at least in the long run of the innovation cycle, the whole market for the novel good can eventually be harvested by the innovator. In the long run and after the disruption of other supply side agents, the benefits that society incurs from adopting the innovation also fall back to the innovator. So, the trade-off is between the expected costs of innovation, which occur at the company level, and the expected long-run benefits of innovation, which occur at a society-wide level, because the society-wide benefit ultimately falls back to the innovator.

The conception of society, as used here, calls for some nuance: society-wide benefits neither mean that they are objectively measurable nor that they are normatively desirable. It only means that if the innovation manages to disrupt all competition, the innovation will be used by the whole society and therefore the innovator profits – until a new disruptor challenges him. Society here means the maximum expansion of agents that want to participate in market processes in which the novelty is exchanged. Note how in this meaning society is contingent and non-institutional. In managerial science, the jargon term is market potential. If new products, services or business models are better than the ones they are about to displace, they will automatically be more attractive; so there are more buyers, market shares or markets, since a wider group of individuals wants to profit from the innovation's benefits and will be willing to purchase the product.

Where does that leave us? The expected cost of innovation at the company level and the expected long-run society-wide benefits of developing new business models stand against the expected costs of innovation at the company level and the expected benefits on the company level of maintaining the established model. If the first trade-off yields more net benefits than the second, then innovation can be expected to be disruptive. But in order for the first trade-off to be more beneficial than the second, time for the novelty to penetrate, capture and eventually disrupt the traditional market is needed. This explains why, on the one hand, insiders are less likely to engage in disruptive innovation. They have more to lose, and they are more accustomed to the company-wide (opposed to the combination of society-wide and company-wide) thinking. On the other hand, it also explains why companies such as Uber or Facebook or smaller startups must be able and willing to operate at a loss for several years. The society-wide benefits can only fall back to the innovator after considerable disruption of the traditional market.

This is the small-scale case for explaining disruptive innovation as a choice and a potential of inventive entrepreneurship. Is there a way of aggregating this trade-off to the macroeconomic scale? No, for this combination of creative destruction and disruptive innovation does not provide a prescriptive or prognostic model. It is still committed to the Schumpeterian idea of creative destruction being about ideas reshaping business models and how their development bears the potential for their own destruction. This destruction often comes at a cost, but it very often leads to overall economic growth and makes people's lives better. Over time and in an empiric claim *ex post*, societies that allow creative destruction to operate grow more productive and richer; their citizens see the benefits of new and better products, shorter work weeks, better jobs and higher living standards.

Two radical examples demonstrating this are the industrial revolution and the ascent of mass accessible information technology. At first, many traditional crafts as well as their jobs were destroyed by the industry. But in the long run, industrialization created more jobs and was able to provide a much broader public with many new and cheaper goods, even of better quality. Similarly, industrialization opened the labor market for more people (including the less skilled) and the supply side to more agents by breaking up the cartel of guilds. In comparison, those countries that disfavored industrialization (France, Spain, Brazil, China) in the late nineteenth century ended up worse off than those that accepted and favored it (the United States, the United Kingdom, Japan) (see Allen 2009).

By the same veneer, mass utilization of information technology, like personal computers or the internet, destroys jobs – think of the old-fashioned typist – and trades – many middlemen. But by making information cheaper and more widely accessible, it makes lives better and provides more opportunities for people to innovate business models and participate in a wide array of activities. Also, countries and sectors adapting more readily to information technology show higher and better welfare effects than others (see Gilpin and Gilpin 2000).

At the end, it is Schumpeter that summarizes it: 'The fundamental impulse that sets and keeps the capitalist engine in motion comes from the new consumers' goods, the new methods of production or transportation, the new markets, the new forms of industrial organization that capitalist enterprise creates' (Schumpeter 1942, p. 83).

3.3 THE CASE OF UBER: IS UBER AN AGENT OF CREATIVE DESTRUCTION?

Is Uber an agent of creative destruction? In the first two sections of this chapter, creative destruction and disruptive innovation were explained in detail. The last section combines them into one view. How does this all apply to Uber? In this section, the question of Uber as an agent of creative destruction is addressed. And so often, where there is creative destruction, there are those who oppose it.

3.3.1   Innovator, Disruptor, Destroyer

> Uber is clearly transforming the taxi business in the United States. But is it disrupting the taxi business? According to the theory, the answer is no. Uber's financial and strategic achievements do not qualify the company as genuinely disruptive – although the company is almost always described that way. Here are two reasons why the label doesn't fit. Disruptive innovations originate in low-end or new-market footholds ... Disruptive innovations don't catch on with mainstream customers until quality catches up to their standards. (Christensen et al. 2015, p. 53)

None other than Christensen himself calls into question Uber's quality as disruptive innovator. Why? There are two ways of explaining Christensen's position. First, this article published in 2015 counters Lepore's 2014 piece. Since the seminal book of 1997, the theory of disruptive innovation has been expanded to incorporate elements like the predictability of success or the difference between innovators' disruption and the development of arrived players. The confluence of the refinement of the theory and the attacks by Lepore might lead Christensen to revise or be overly strict with some cases.

But there is a second and more substantial answer. Christensen is wrong about Uber's business model. As analysed in Chapter 2, Uber bases its innovation on technology, which is the necessary condition for being a disruptive innovator. This isn't called into question by Christensen. Also, Uber fulfills many of the sufficient conditions like developing new markets, marketing the new idea or acquiring new targets. Also, this is not criticized by Christensen. The problem is whether it originated in the low end of the market or in new market footholds. Christensen claims not. If Uber were a limousine company, Christensen's critique might be right. But that is exactly not the case. Uber is an intermediary that uses technology to match supply and demand. By doing so, Uber provides a service that is a substitute for taxi rides, cheaper than them, more comfortable, often in cars of higher quality and a source of entrepreneurship for drivers with spare capacity. Seeing Uber as an intermediary diminishing costs and optimizing capacity puts it at the low end of markets. And it is through this intermediation that the quality of Uber's services quickly caught up with the taxicab industry. So, Christensen's second critique is also dismissed.

Is Uber an agent of creative destruction after all? Its business model seems revolutionary, but is also consistent with the claim that it is ideas that stand behind disruptive innovation. Uber can be presented as a convergence of two – in the end – simple ideas. The first: selling unused or underused capacity. This is already the case in many different markets, such as for cargo spots on trains, ships and planes, but also for hotel rooms, harvest and agricultural goods. The second is transferring the market mechanism to an online, real-time auctioning system. The real-time auctioning system is also already the case in eBay, for example, a market for virtually everything. And the same principle is being expanded to human resources, dining, hospitals and, maybe literally, a myriad of things. Combining both ideas through intermediation, Uber creates something perceived as new.

Uber expects society-wide benefits of its services falling back to the company in the long run. For this to materialize, a substantial portion of the taxicab industry must be disrupted. With its 'noisy market entry' and celebrity endorsement, Uber is also innovative in marketing. In fact, Uber was innovative on a number of different levels. And so, Uber's business starts to disrupt the traditional market for taxicab companies. It is too early to tell if Uber will succeed in completely transforming or destroying it.

It might be worthwhile to remember that the combination of these ideas has been practiced before Uber, and in the very same market. ZabCab, for example, was an application developed with the aim of hailing cabs at market price, with the possibility of real-time auctioning free capacity. In Germany, one of the first countries where charges have been pressed against Uber, a non-taxicab ride-sharing service was established as early as the 1980s without any opposition and regulatory response: the *Mitfahrtzentrale*. Anyone travelling in a car with free seats can pool the ride. Normally, this service is used by people travelling further distances, and the drivers do not generate profits, merely cover their expenses (Schmitt and Sommer 2013).

The potential for disruption in Uber's business model is large. Hailing virtually anyone with a free seat at real-time market price, turning virtually everyone into a for-profit driver, allowing people to make a profit out of sharing free, unused capacity is not only for Uber itself a beneficial idea. Other sectors can easily copy it. Uber as the 'outsider' realized that the trade-off between its costs and the society-wide benefits that would eventually fall back to the company is more beneficial than the traditional trade-off. The disruptive innovation launched by Uber was to turn every underused capacity into a potential for-profit taxi. The creative destruction it entails – but did not fully unleash – is the end of regulated taxis and therefore the end of regulated taxi companies, or: the end of the regulated taxi market. If the Uberization thesis is correct (see Chapter 2), this creative destruction goes even beyond that.

So yes, Uber is a disruptive innovator and as such an agent of creative destruction. It does not become an agent because any entity named creative destruction called Uber to be its agent nor because there is a covering law stating that every now and then creative destruction happens. Being its agent is nothing more than one among other consequences of Uber's innovative entrepreneurialism. Will this disruption or even destruction come to a halt? Schumpeter says 'nobody ever is an entrepreneur all the time, and nobody ever can be only an entrepreneur' (1939, p. 102). And this is a serious preoccupation. What could stop Uber's disruption? There are internal factors that qualify. For example, bad management ideas, stagnation, loss of productivity and innovation. But there are also external factors, such as regulation, that are strong candidates for halting Uber's innovation.

3.3.2   Stopping Creative Destruction

Activities against Uber are abundant. Private parties, very often Uber's competition, try to stop it from continuing and disrupting their business. Often, these private agents stopping Uber's creative destruction are successful.

Private activities against Uber are actions of private, non-state agents. These actions are mainly taken by Uber's competitors through the usual regulatory framework like the justice system. However, many actions are also loud demonstrations on the streets and the blockage of Uber's services. There are different non-state agents with different motivations for their actions against Uber. In different places of the globe, traditional taxicab companies are bitter against the low-end market entrant. Note, however, that most of these taxicab companies do not object to the idea of technology helping clients to find free cars. Most of the protesting taxi companies even have similar applications of their own. Also, they claim not to be afraid of competition. Some taxicab companies even claim to be taking a so-called pro-competitive stance; 'Competition is good, as long as all are regulated equally.'

The anti-Uber camp also consists of labor unionists who fear for their jobs. They attack Uber, saying that the company stands for a particularly extreme form of wage dumping that refuses to allow for any minimum wage. There are also private agents concerned with safety, insurance and general consumer protection.

The reactions of the non-state agents exemplify the different points made in this chapter. When Schumpeter speculates that other companies will be destroyed by the innovator, that people might lose their jobs or even that the 'system' might collapse, he is proved right by the fears of the anti-Uber protesters: taxi companies fearing their destruction by the less cost-intensive, technologically-savvy competitor, labor unions fearing the loss of workplaces (not just their rearrangement, since if everyone with spare capacity can turn into a taxi driver, the very profession of the driver might become obsolete), and even consumer protection entities fearing that their preferred type of consumer protection (and therefore their own legitimacy as such entities) might disappear.

But the most interesting arguments of these non-state agents against Uber are the so-called pro-competitive arguments. They reason that competition is fine, as long as all are regulated equally. It is important to scrutinize this argument a little more closely since it entails that regulation can be a pro-competitive force, or even that the regulation of competition in markets has benefits for all market agents.

Here are some examples of different private attempts at stopping Uber around the globe, as of May 2016:[5]

- *San Francisco*: in 2015, taxi drivers protested outside Uber's headquarters when attendees of the US Conference of Mayors took a tour of the company's Market Street office.
- *California*: in her decision, chief administrative law judge Karen V. Clopton of the California Public Utilities Commission contended that Uber has not complied with state laws designed to ensure that drivers are doling out rides fairly to all passengers, regardless of where they live or who they are. She said Uber's months-long refusal to provide such data is in violation of the 2013 law that legalized ride-hailing firms. She recommended that the ride-sharing giant be fined 7.3 million dollars and be suspended from operating in California.
- *Paris*: French taxi drivers smashed cars, lit fires and blocked highways as part of a nationwide taxi strike specifically aimed at Uber in 2014. The drivers object to UberPOP, the company's cheapest service in France.
- *London*: drivers of the famous black cabs have argued that Uber bypasses local licensing and safety laws and amounts to unfair competition. They have staged a number of high-profile protests in 2013, 2014 and 2015, including go-slow demonstrations that have brought traffic in the center of London to a standstill. The taxi

drivers' slogan was 'enforce the law.' London's transport chiefs, as a reaction, announced plans to tighten control on private hire vehicles.

- *Toronto*: the Toronto City council voted on changes to taxi regulations that regulate ride-hailing app services like Uber. The city's taxi drivers attended the public hearings wearing yellow T-shirts.
- *Sao Paulo*: taxi drivers demonstrated outside the chamber of deputies of Sao Paulo, Brazil, against the use of the Uber application in the country. The demonstration was called by the Brazilian association of taxi unions.
- *Rome*: hundreds of taxis took to the streets in Rome to protest against a law proposal allowing Uber to introduce UberPOP to Italy. That service employs drivers without the special licenses normally required to drive a taxi.
- *Melbourne*: taxi companies deployed their fleets to block the streets of the Australian metropole. They deplored the 'unfair competition' that has been tolerated by the city.
- *Brussels*: taxi drivers started to write on their vehicles '*ceci n'est pas un taxi clandestin*' ('This is not a clandestine taxi').
- *Mexico*: the National Forum of Taxi Drivers announced an alliance with other taxi associations in Central America and Colombia to 'declare war' on Uber.
- *Chicago*: taxi drivers refused to pick up fares during anti-Uber protests.
- *Detroit*: taxi drivers and enterprises stated that 'Uber and similar companies should be under the same regulations as cabbies,' also claiming that the taxicabs' business had declined up to 70 percent in the downtown area since the ride-sharing services became popular. The result is less traditional taxis but also less service, especially during non-peak hours. While taxis must maintain a certain service level because of city statutes, non-regulated entities, like Uber, do not. This leads to a shortage of cabs.
- *Miami*: taxi drivers and companies organized protests in order to increase public awareness of the different regulatory framework under which they and Uber operate. Also, their main case is about public safety. They claim Uber would endanger public safety.
- Other protests took place in *Los Angeles, Houston, Dallas, Kansas City, Seattle, Philadelphia, Boston, Washington DC*, among others.
- *Atlanta*: in September 2014, a class action was filed by Atlanta taxicab drivers against Uber and all of its drivers in the Superior Court of Fulton County, Georgia, for restitution of all metered fares

collected via the Uber and UberX apps for trips originating within the Atlanta city limits.
- *Philadelphia*: in December 2014, Checker Cab Philadelphia and 44 other taxi companies in Philadelphia, Pennsylvania filed a lawsuit in the Federal Court of the Eastern District of Pennsylvania, alleging that Uber was operating illegally in the city.

But Uber – or Uber drivers – also counteract (in the year 2015):

- *New York*: Uber staged a protest outside New York City Hall, where inside members of the City Council Transportation Committee were introducing a bill that would require the Taxi and Limousine Commission to limit the issuance of new for-hire vehicle licenses. The law would mean Uber could only add about 200 new drivers to the service in New York over the years. More specifically, transportation companies would be limited to adding new drivers at a rate that amounts to 1 percent of the number of drivers currently on each company's platform in New York City. This cap would severely limit the growth of transportation companies in New York City, and would be a big win for the taxi industry. In an email to its clients, Uber stated: 'We need your help. Mayor de Blasio is supporting a bill that would stop thousands of new drivers from joining the Uber platform. This bill would destroy 10,000 job opportunities for New Yorkers in just one year, and result in longer wait times, higher prices and less reliable service for riders.'
- *Sao Paulo*: after the banning of Uber in Sao Paulo, Brazil (see above), many drivers and customers protested for the service.
- *Toronto*: after the adjustment of the city statute on cabs, Uber riders and driver-partners united in front of City Hall to rally support for Uber in Toronto.
- *London*: as a result of the protests mentioned above, Transport for London has proposed new regulation that would ban the key features of the Uber mini-cab service. The new proposals would force a minimum five minute wait between ordering a car and it picking you up, and would ban the company from using its phone application to show users whether there is a taxi ready nearby. The consultation document, which purports to make the changes to ensure London has 'an effective and up to date regulatory system' would also force Uber to take bookings up to seven days in advance and employ its drivers full time. Uber gathered 80,000 signatures in a petition to rescind the law.

This merely indicative list of examples shows that there are different ways to counter Uber. But in most of them, private resort to applying regulation of Uber is used because it is known or expected that regulation will stop the disruption created by Uber. Even if it is not the regulation's task to curb creative destruction, it is exactly what less innovative incumbents expect it to do.

One of the most interesting cases against Uber was in Germany. There are three twists that make it interesting. First, the case was brought not by just a taxi competitor but by a competitor technology platform for sharing car rides. Second, the argumentation was the most developed case for an economics of regulations. Third, it shows the legal complexity of most court cases. It is worthwhile to look deeper into it. The case against Uber was brought forward by the Taxi Deutschland Service-gesellschaft, which offers a rival application that links users to registered taxi drivers. The company argued that Uber was not operating a legitimate service because its drivers did not have the correct permits, were not properly insured and were not subject to checks. German law allows drivers without a commercial license to pick up passengers only if they charge no more than the operating cost of the trip; only the Passenger Transportation Act[6] mandate permits the transport of people commercially and if there is any commercial intent behind a service provider, it must be registered under this law. There are further frame-works to be applied at a nationwide as well as at local levels. Generally, there are rules regarding technical safety, consumer safety, consumer information, accreditation and routes. These rules can be very fine-grained, for example, stating that a taxi from a city cannot pick up clients in another city unless the client in the other city has called the specific 'foreign' car (whereby the term 'called' should be taken literally, since hailing is not considered calling, and clicking on an app does not fulfill the semantic denotation either; in short, calling means using the phone).

The main idea behind this rule is to assure a certain local market for local taxi drivers and to incentivize the provision of taxi services in smaller cities. There are many other rationalizations for these types of rules, for example, the argument that only local drivers know local streets (with some validity before the advent of the GPS). Another good example of regulation is the unification of fares in a given geographic context. The reasoning behind this is that the customer cannot know *ex ante* how much each taxi company charges, so the consumer cannot make an educated choice. Therefore, competition among taxis should take place over service and not price (with less validity, even before the age of information technology, since competition always has a price com-ponent). Of course, this legal framework is around 50 years old. There is also much concern about insurance and minimum wages.

What was the result? The first court decision to ban Uber in 2014, a local court in Frankfurt, was lifted by a higher court on the grounds that Taxi Deutschland simply failed to file its claim by the cut-off date. The merits of Taxi Deutschland's case were not considered by the judge, and the court did not make any judgment on whether or not Uber's services are legal in Germany, although a spokesman for the Frankfurt Regional Court confirmed that the judges were sympathetic to Taxi Deutschland's argument that the service competes unfairly with local taxis. Local courts in Berlin and Hamburg have repeatedly banned the company in their respective cities. The courts determined that Uber's drivers did not comply with German law for the commercial transportation of passengers. The Berlin court said that there is no way of telling whether private drivers using the mobile phone application are fit for the special responsibility of carrying passengers. It also said that some Uber services would fall between regulations for taxi and rental car services. Since then, further bans and ban lifts have followed.

To sum up, Uber can be an agent of creative destruction. This means, Uber's business model is disruptive enough to change the taxicab industry – among others – forever. Many incumbents in that industry want to stop this disruption. They chiefly use actual regulation for doing so. Their main argument goes along this line: 'If it is not subject to the same regulation, it should not operate.' But the list above shows that Uber itself in answering these private actions often adapts to regulation. Just not to the exact taxicab regulation that its competitors demand. The clear-cut disruptor in the Schumpeterian sense would not stop disrupting until the entire traditional industry is destroyed and the innovators can carry all the benefits from destruction. Uber does not behave that way. It is open to some degree of regulation, even if it stops innovation. This anomaly is studied in Chapter 4 and in the Conclusion.

There are not only private actions against Uber. As Chapter 2 mentions and the list above suggests, state agents also demonstrate a keen interest in regulating Uber. And this too is studied in Chapter 4.

SUMMARY

What are creative destruction and disruptive innovation? Creative destruction is the overall process of change and adaptation of actual industries to novelties. Many traditional business models are driven out of the market processes by new technology, new forms of production, new marketing and new business models. Disruptive innovation is primarily technology-backed innovation starting at the low end of markets or creating a new market foothold. This innovation changes the whole character of market processes in which it is exchanged. It makes it impossible for the marker processes to exist without it. Both are open-textured processes with non-determinate and no determinable possible outcomes. If a specific innovation was disruptive and if it creatively destroyed any industry can often only be stated during the process and not at its beginning.

Is Uber an agent of creative destruction? Uber's business model innovates on different levels. It lowers costs, it increases quality, it optimizes idle capacity and it has 'flashy' marketing. If that is enough to destroy the whole taxicab industry remains to be seen. Actually, it is unfolding disruptive energy and many taxicab providers have already adapted their value propositions to include many of Uber's elements (app, rating, surveillance, among others). But because of this disruptive energy, many incumbent taxicab companies are trying to stop Uber by using regulation. It is not the task of regulation to stop innovation, but that is what Uber's competition expects it to do.

NOTES

1. One of the consequences of understanding the Austrian School in Economics as a series of family resemblances is that it is difficult to account for to what extent a particular economist is part of that School. Therefore, if here it is stated that Schumpeter was loosely affiliated to Austrianism, it does not mean that he wouldn't consider him one and it shouldn't mean that he was more closely affiliated to any other body of theories in economics. It just means that his theoretical work does not show all elements of Austrianism identified in Chapter 1. But then again, most Austrians don't subscribe to that list in its entirety. This is one reason for the claim that Austrian economics is better understood as a heterodox position full of heterodoxies.
2. Which, in this case, is a multiplication of probabilities.
3. Veblen was an important economist and sociologist of his time. Although many of his contributions to both fields are still used today, his name was quickly forgotten. Veblen's main contributions were the conceptions of conspicuous consumption and conspicuous leisure, which are performed to demonstrate wealth or mark social status. He is also considered the founder of institutional economics, which claims that all economics is also dependent on the institutions of society. As a leading intellectual of the Progressive Era in the Unites States, Veblen attacked production for profit. His emphasis on conspicuous consumption greatly influenced the socialist thinkers who sought a non-Marxist critique of capitalism. Unlike Schumpeter, Veblen believed that technology would (not could) lead mankind to socialism. And unlike Schumpeter, Veblen liked that idea (Diggins 1978, p. 84).
4. Scientific management revolutionized industrial manufacturing in the early twentieth century. It was concerned primarily with the physical efficiency of an individual worker. Scientific management is based on the work of the US engineer Frederick Winslow Taylor (1856–1915) who in his 1911 book *The Principles of Scientific Management* laid down the fundamental principles of large-scale manufacturing through assembly-line factories. It

emphasizes rationalization and standardization of work through the division of labor, time and motion studies, work measurement and piece-rate wages.

5. This is a non-exhaustive list of examples compiled by roaming on the internet. It is not the goal of this list to be complete, but to provide a brief overview on the different, global actions against Uber by its competitors.

6. Personenbeförderungsgesetz (PBefG), Personenbeförderungsgesetz vom 21. März 1961 (BGBl. I S. 241), das zuletzt durch Artikel 2 Absatz 147 des Gesetzes vom 7. August 2013 (BGBl. I S. 3154) geändert worden ist.

4. Are innovation and regulation opposites?

While creative destruction and disruptive innovation change the entrepreneurial landscape, regulation, especially regulation of sectorial markets and competition regulation, delay this change or even bring it to a halt. Chapter 3 dealt with the conceptions of creative destruction and disruptive innovation. They are non-teleological, undetermined processes with a considerable amount of spontaneity, or even chaos.[1] In the present chapter, the focus will be regulation. In the first section, the economics of so-called pro-competition regulation is discussed. In the second section, the economics of competition regulation is explored. Following the same structure as previous chapters, the third section applies this to Uber asking the question if Uber is changing its business model to accommodate regulation.

As in the other chapters, this chapter sees markets as a series of open-ended, undetermined processes. The outcomes of market processes cannot be calculated beforehand and cannot be judged by an objective stand. Their desirability is a matter for the different agents to assess individually. Most of the time, most regulation does not want to directly impact the outcomes of markets. Usually, regulation just wants to set the rules for markets. According to the logic behind regulation, market agents are free to engage or not as long as they act in conformity with the rules – that are the same for everyone. This seems a very straightforward claim. However, it is not. For the claim implies that rules are constitutive to markets. And it further implies that the rules do not emerge from the consensus of the market agents, but is given to them by design by the regulator. This contradicts much of the view on market processes explained in Chapter 1. How much it contradicts the market process approach will be explained in depth.

There is another facet of regulation that at least raises some suspicion. It is neither its aim nor its task to curb or stop innovation or creative destruction. But many private agents use regulation against Uber for precisely that end. These agents recognized that regulation has at least a detrimental effect on disruptive innovation. Possibly, this detrimental effect not only touches disruption but all innovation.

There are two caveats applying to this chapter. First, it is not supposed to debunk all regulation, but the specific regulation being studied here, which is sectorial regulation and competition regulation. Second, the chapter is not about all regulation and all political desiderata. It is about the effects of some types of regulation on innovation and creative destruction in market processes. It might be that there is a social need to ban Uber.[2] But even if that were the case, it is outside the scope of this chapter and this book. The only question that is addressed here is: from the point of view of the market as a process of spontaneous exchanges, does regulation affect innovation positively or negatively, if at all? This question will be explored using the case study of Uber. And it will be explored according to the logic of innovation and the economics behind it.

4.1 THE DILEMMA OF PRO-COMPETITIVE REGULATION

'Competition is fine as long as all are regulated equally' was one of the arguments used by Uber's competitors when calling for bans or regulation of Uber. This view has many sympathizers and it is one of the main motivations for state agents to regulate certain – if not all – markets: taxicabs and food processing, hotels and consulting. Usually, this type of 'pro-competitive' regulation is about the conditions for market entry and operation. It is time to look at how competitive pro-competitive regulation is.

4.1.1 Level Playing Field

There are two so-called pro-competitive arguments. First, equal regulation for all agents of a sector guarantees the equal chances of all agents. Even if regulation leads to more fixed costs, if regulation is the same for all, the level of fixed costs will be roughly the same for all market participants. According to this logic, competition will become competition in terms of lower operating costs, better quality of services and the serviced network. This is the classical 'level playing field' argument. The second so-called pro-competitive argument is that in most places, regulation legitimizes those businesses operating under it. In other words, regulation is used as a tool for marketing and public relations for taxi companies, as explained later in this section. *Time Magazine* (2014) wrote: 'New York taxis used to have a reputation for smelly cars, ripped seats and eccentric drivers. Today, New York cabs are nearly all clean and well maintained. Drivers don't usually say much unprompted. The cabs feel safe.' In other words, many taxi companies are afraid that Uber will bring shame back into the business and that they will generally fall victim to it. Furthermore, this second string of argumentation reasons that if there are incentives for a low-quality supply of services, this supply will be of minimum quality. This is the 'sectorial quality' argument.

Both arguments appeal to a simple intuition, and it is difficult to refute them at that level. The intuition is that if something is regulated, it is safe, it has quality and it is trustworthy. There is even another intuition, almost epiphenomenal to the first; if a market is equally regulated, it is fair. However, both, the 'level playing field' as well as the 'sectorial quality' arguments are flawed in their inner economic logic as well as in the very idea behind them.

The 'level playing field' argument assumes that regulation and regulation-induced costs are exogenous and homogeneous. Exogeneity means that something completely outside the individual firm's realm and influence affects the firm. In a stronger sense, exogenous factors impact on economic agents without their prior knowledge. In this case, economic agents cannot even anticipate the impact of those factors, that is, cannot prepare for them. Homogeneity denotes the property of regulation-induced costs to affect all regulated firms equally. Homogeneity of regulation-induced costs comes from the necessary property of homogeneous regulation, that is, a regulatory sentence is not directed toward just one or some firms but to all firms in the relevant sector. Therefore, regulation and regulation-induced costs affect all relevant firms in similar ways.

It is evident that regulation and regulation-induced costs cannot hold the stronger concept of exogeneity. If these regulations and their costs were completely exogenous, they would impact taxi companies without their prior knowledge, and the companies would have to deal with them practically as surprises to which they can adjust. However, most taxi regulations are set up and developed in dialogue with the local taxi industry. Taking this dialogic development of regulation into account, not even the weaker sense of exogeneity applies. Taxi firms not only know about regulation and its development but they actively influence it. This is in the nature of the policy dialogue.

It is irrelevant how the regulatory body of the specific industry, taxicabs, is formally organized. As long as there is mandatory regulation or a regulatory monopoly, all arguments developed here apply to the different institutional forms of regulators, be they the legislative as regulator, a separate industry-specific regulator body or even a self-regulation body formed by the sector. If, however, there is a voluntary regulation or overlapping regulators in competition to each other, there is at least some exposure to the positive dynamics of market processes.

The norm is, however, that there is mandatory regulation and one regulator. In most taxicab jurisdictions, the regulatory body stands in dialogue with the regulated sector. Per se, a dialogue has to be open to the influence of the regulated industry because it is necessarily conceived as a two-way communication. And since the dialogue is about regulation as well as the regulation itself is also a political act, the very process of regulating is open for lobbying activities. The reference to dialogue is in this case intentionally open and embraces different types of participation of regulated firms and other stakeholders in the process of regulation. Forms of dialogue are, for example, stakeholder consultation, hearings, fora for regulators and their respective sectors and regulatory bodies with the presence of people affiliated or formerly affiliated to the regulated industry. These forms of dialogue are necessary for the regulator since it needs some knowledge of the regulated sector and it can only gain this knowledge from firsthand experience in the sector itself. A regulator that would not engage in exchange with the regulated industry would be so far away from the industry's reality that its regulatory activity would either not impact the industry or not be efficient. Dialogue is necessary for industry or sectorial regulation (Flohr 2014; OECD 2014).

As necessary as different forms of dialogue between regulator and regulated industry are for regulation itself, they enable regulatory arbitrage[3] among the taxi companies. Companies with more means for lobbying or companies with better arguments will try to influence regulation and regulators in their favor. The policy dialogue makes it possible for regulators to grant special consideration to the industry's needs – or to a single company's needs – even if those needs are detrimental to the very aim of the regulation (assuming, just for the sake of this argument that there is an economically sound reason behind the aim of regulation). This can happen even without bad faith on either part. In accepting their arguments, which is in the nature of dialogue, regulators are giving some stakeholders leverage over others.

It might seem odd to amalgamate three phenomena that are normally perceived as independent from each other: dialogue, lobbying and argumentative engagement. Naturally, they are different. Dialogue has an open texture, lobbying is often about the advancement of particular or vested interests and good arguments might advance the regulator's understanding of the market. Also, it might seem odd to argue for a detrimental character of good arguments in the process of regulation and its implementation. However, from the point of view of exogeneity, these three are similar for they transform the character of regulation. Through dialogue, lobby and/or argumentative engagement, regulation and regulation-induced costs are influenced by the subjects of regulation themselves. While the pro-competitive advocates might want a competition over products, they are also creating a competition over influencing regulation. This contradicts the motto that competition is good as long as all are being regulated equally, for not all participants are. So, regulation and regulation-induced costs are not (completely) exogenous to (all) taxi companies.

A major form of leverage of some agents over others is regulatory capture. It is the process by which regulatory agencies eventually come to be dominated by the very industries they were charged with regulating. Regulatory capture happens when a regulatory agency, formed to act in the public's interest, eventually acts in ways that benefit the industry it is supposed to be regulating, rather than the public (Veltrop and de Haan 2014). Not all dialogue, lobbying and argumentative engagement leads to regulatory capture, but even minor influencing of the regulatory bodies diminishes the exogenous character of regulation and regulation-induced costs. Diminishing exogeneity automatically leads to an unlevelling of the playing field. Even if there were no dialogue, regulation still remains a political act or at least an act with some political relevance. And even the regulatory body that does not engage in dialogue with the regulated industry has an institutional behavior that is used by the subjects of regulation as hints on the content of regulation. The political act itself might be influenced by other factors.

But that is enough discussion on this first property of the 'level playing field' argument. It mistakenly assumes that regulation impacts its subjects without their influence. It is time to turn to the second property, to homogeneity.

Even if taxicab regulations were exogenous, it would not follow that they would impact on all taxi companies alike, since the regulated companies are not homogeneous. They differ substantially among each other and so differs the impact of regulation on them. The same regulation impacts companies differently, depending at least on their size, their specific business model and the structure of their business. Even if regulation is homogeneous at issuance, the costs it creates are heterogeneous at absorption, that is, at their implementation by the single taxi company. Usually, their impact on well-established, larger agents is smaller than on smaller or newer agents. Also, regulation-induced costs set up market entrance barriers in terms of regulation complexity and costs. With high barriers to market entrance, cheaper but also more innovative services are discouraged from entering the market. Also, traditional companies are discouraged from innovating because they can rely on the market entrance barriers. This discouragement not only refers to innovation but to competition as a whole. The combination of capped supply, territorial hegemony, diminished possibilities of lowering costs and stable or rising demand means that single providers do not need to do better than the regulation, the one they influenced, want them to. They don't need to compete over prices nor over quality because demand has no other option but them. So, in reality, regulation itself dampens competition; furthermore, it distorts the playing field through regulation-induced costs, discourages innovation and discourages price and quality competition (Boyer 1987; Cicala 2014; Cochrane 2014). In the end, regulation dampens competition and decreases efficiency in specific market processes.

By its inner logic, the 'level playing field' argument fails to provide such since it is trapped in a dilemma: if it applies uniform regulation uniformly to a given industry, it impacts the individual firms differently, since they are different; if it applies differentiated regulation according to individual firms, it comes at the cost of uniform regulation, on which its intuitive appeal to fairness is grounded. The high market entry barriers are just another example of how the 'level playing field' argument makes the field even more uneven.

However, it is not necessary to solve this dilemma, since the very idea behind the 'level playing field' argument is at fault. In order to understand the fundamental mistake of its logic, it is useful to take it with some essentialism: if a level playing field is something necessary for a specific sector, then why constrain this level playing field principle just to the regulatory environment of that specific sector? Usually, level playing field arguments defend themselves by invoking fairness and efficiency. Economically, they would be making the point that the respective market does not work efficiently without regulation. Logically, and if there is a lack of efficiency in the market, why not claim a level playing field regarding the organization of all market agents, that is, companies, as well? Through this, aforementioned distortions of the market could even be avoided. But it follows from here that the complete homogenization of the regulatory environment as well as of the market agents could deliver more efficient results. If that is the case, then a single monopolistic supplier could be the most efficient way to organize this market. Those who embark on the level playing field logic are on the path of reclaiming a monopolistic organization of the market (Epstein 2005; Knoll 2007). The problems with this argument can be taken even further in those jurisdictions with a unitary price – like Germany (see Chapter 3). The fundamental challenge faced by this argument is as follows: if there is a need for equal regulations and equal prices, why is there a need for multiple providers? If there is a need for a single price, and if there is a need for uniform service levels, insurance, wages, why then is there a need for a market at all?

In as far as the level playing field claims for uniform inputs, it embarks on the logic of uniform outputs. As such, it is far from a pro-competitive argument. It is, in fact, an argument for collectivization.

4.1.2 Sectorial Quality

Now, to the second so-called pro-competitive argument: The 'sectorial quality' argument assumes that only government-induced regulation can guarantee a minimum standard of quality (including insurance, safety and hygiene). Most importantly, by guaranteeing these minimum standards, regulation is legitimizing the regulated sector and its companies. This legitimization can be used by them in their communications with customers and suppliers, among others.

Government-induced quality regulation can be managed directly by the state, by a state agent, by an independent agency or even by the sector itself (in which case it is misleadingly called self-regulation). But as long as it is a mandatory regulation, it maintains the same character of direct state intervention without the alternative for the regulated companies.

Proponents of the 'sectorial quality' argument necessarily believe the 'level playing field' argument. But in addition to it, they want, in the name of competition, a more robust regulation of the service per se. As a consequence, they claim that if the state sets the minimum criteria for a sector, the whole sector profits from the effect of this intervention. This profit occurs twofold. First, those companies that cannot and do not wish to comply must cease their economic activities; this solidifies the position of the incumbents. Second and more importantly, the state endorses the incumbent companies by labelling them as compliant, or qualitative. By being regulated, the industry is also being legitimized. This occurs at least in the strong version of the argument. A weaker version would be that the sector complying with the minimum standards of quality can advertise for them. In this case, sectorial quality regulation is a marketing or public relations tool for a given industry. In its logic, this second version is weaker because the sector is not legitimized or endorsed by the state; it just uses state regulation as a tool. However, it is in this second version of the argument that the threat of regulatory capture becomes most apparent. In this version, regulation is just understood as a tool for marketing and public relations. It is in the nature of the sector to maximize the range and use of this tool.

But is the 'sectorial quality' argument pro-competitive, as claimed by state agents and taxicab companies against Uber? It is not because in calling for a central and governmental regulation, it disregards at least two alternatives.

First, there is a possibility of voluntary sectorial self-regulation and even the competition among different sectorial self-regulations, that is, the overlapping of different initiatives for quality in a given industry. It is, for example, conceivable that some taxi companies would voluntarily agree on minimum quality criteria and enforce them. They could launch a quality standard as a label and market it. So each company adhering to this standard could advertise it. If a company fails to implement the standard, it cannot use the label in its communication any more. It is also as easily conceivable that more than just one quality standard is developed in the taxi industry and that the existing labels compete against each other. In order for this system to work, adhesion should be completely voluntary and the standard setters would be able to exclude members. Legally speaking, this also entails that some cartels – the companies committed to quality standards are formally a cartel – have positive overall outcomes. So competition regulation would have to respect this competition over quality too. On another note, this concept of competing standards of quality can easily be embraced by consumers and other stakeholders like labor unions. So, it is possible that consumers launch their own quality label or labels or that the taxi company-driven labels invite consumers and other stakeholders to judge quality. There are different forms of voluntary cooperation based on competition that could increase the quality of a sector (see, for example, Sunder 2002).

Even without a system of competing labels with minimum standards, there is still a second alternative to state regulation, and this is the plain competition over quality. Recalling the first chapter of the book, quality can be one of the value propositions in firms' strategy, so why not accept a differentiation through it? Hotels are an example of competition over quality. With the star rating, the diamond rating and different internet portals for guest feedback, good hotels are differentiated from bad ones with a positive outcome for the whole industry. And all these systems are largely voluntary (Wu and Yong 2013). In Switzerland, for example, there are two competing quality labels for hotels, that is, two competing systems of star-classification (Cser and Ohuchi 2008).

Similarly, Uber lets customers rate their experience, and these ratings are published transparently. This leads to differentiation between Uber and other mobility services, but also among Uber drivers themselves. And there is also a voluntary level of quality and self-regulation, which is in the best business interest of an expanding company. In addition, questions of insurance and safety are settled by the market processes as such. Uber insures the passengers simply because it has too much to lose if accidents happen.

The 'sectorial quality' argument, in calling for direct government regulation, disregards possible economic alternatives that might be more efficient. It especially disregards competition. As such, it is not a pro-competitive argument. Because of its disregard of competition and because of its preference for the state as legitimizing a stance, the argument is not an economic argument at all, but a purely normative one. And in its normative sense, in implying that only though government regulation an industry can offer quality, it also implies that a monopolistic industry under the auspices, guidance or even direct management of government would work best altogether. The fundamental challenge faced by this argument is as follows: if there is a need for uniform quality, why is there a need for multiple providers? Why is there a need for markets? In this case, it is the same fault in its inner logic as in the 'level playing field' argument; just an even more robust mistake.

Both the 'level playing field' and the 'sectorial quality' arguments diminish competition because they follow an anti-competitive logic. They distort market processes at the level of their input as well as output. Also, the reasoning of both arguments leads to the conclusion that in the industry to which they are applied, market processes and competition are neither necessary at all nor the most efficient form of market organization. In fact, both arguments have the logic that central planning is more effective than the market as an organizational principle. This might lead to the question of why to tolerate market processes at all? In their reasoning the following thesis arises: if the input and the result of the market process are to be regulated, then the market as such is not needed.[4]

4.2   THE CONUNDRUM OF COMPETITION REGULATION

There is more than just the regulation of market entry and operation in the state agents' toolboxes. There is also the regulation of competitive behavior per se. This is called competition regulation. State agents explicitly claim that competition regulation has positive effects on overall welfare. Implicitly, they are claiming to know what is better for the future, the industry, consumers, employees and society at large. And this is what this section reviews. What is the economics behind competition regulation and does it really help the market processes?

On the one hand, the market processes must be free, but on the other, there seems to be a demand for rules within this freedom. The following will show that those rules regarded as competition regulation are not up to protecting or supporting the market processes in their diversity. On the contrary, competition regulation impedes the market processes from freely unfolding. The problems associated with competition regulation can easily be ascribed to two excessive demands on the issue: Competition regulation first overtaxes the idea of the market per se and overstrains economic theory, and second, expects too much of the regulators, personally and institutionally. Excessive demands, in the above sense, mean competition regulation generally presupposes or expects too much and has a far too high opinion of itself.

4.2.1 Problems with Models

Competition regulation relies on models of markets-as-institutions and welfare. And the problems begin: the object of competition regulation is competition – and not market processes. Textbooks like Posner (2009), Neef (2008), Zäch (2005) or Motta (2004) bear witness to this declared definition.[5] However, both terms are often nonchalantly used as synonyms, which they are not. Very seldom are they used as opposites, which they also are not but can be, at times. Markets, understood as a series of processes and as an organizational principle, are different from competition as the normative outcome of a given institutional market.

Competition is a condition of the market process, namely, the condition of competing buyers and suppliers who challenge themselves and each other in order to be better, more reasonably priced or both. Alternatively, competition can be understood as a process of discovery and freedom of action by not consciously taking place between competitors, but arising from (largely unforeseeable) technological innovations and entrepreneurial initiative. However, this is not the conception of competition favored by the theory of competition regulation. Competition regulation regards perfect competition as the state in which markets should be. Ensuring that the market remains in the condition of perfect competition is the goal and task of competition regulation (Posner 2009). Perfect competition means that the behavior of the individual agent in the market does not influence the market.[6] That is quite the contrary of what market processes are.

In order to understand the difference between the idea of competition regulation and the nature of market processes, some of the characteristics of the market processes, as outlined in Chapter 1, should be recalled. The term market is just an abbreviation denoting a whole conglomerate of processes, interactions and exchanges between individual entities that engage therein freely and without *ex ante* central coordination. Alternatively, the term market refers to an organizational principle allowing individuals to engage in these processes, interactions and exchanges. In any case, the market is about people and firms, individual entities: market processes are the continuous revelation of individual and collective preferences, means-ends calculations, assessments (of the self and the others) and information stock by its agents, that is, free individual entities. As such, market processes are necessarily open-ended and undeterminate. The outcomes of these processes (prices and quantities) are only temporary aggregate information about these revealed preferences. The outcomes of markets have no other quality than being aggregate bearers of information (Schneider 2014). Understood as such a process, markets can have different but only temporary conditions. Among these conditions, competition is certainly one, but market processes also allow voluntary cooperations, monopolies, oligopolies and the like. In this conception of the market, monopolies and oligopolies are extremely unstable conditions. Should a monopolist misuse his position under market conditions, he will not be able to hold it for long because the other agents either will form competition or will substitute the good being provided by these monopolies and oligopolies. Of course, this element does not work when oligopolies and monopolies are protected by legal framework, as is the case in the taxicab sector. In addition, there are market conditions not categorized under any term, be they monopolistic competition, cooperative associations or surrogate competition, for example.

It is inherent to the market processes that none of its conditions are static, and therefore no condition can be guaranteed or even preferred. As long as market entry is not legally or improperly prevented, all conditions are 'perfect,' whereby 'perfect' means in principle open for the further development of market processes. In other words, market processes develop without the need of a 'level playing field' or the per-established condition of competition. What begins as a monopoly today may (depending on the behavior of the other market participants) be subject to competition tomorrow – or not be on the market anymore because buyers are finding substitutes or are simply not interested in the product. 'Free market,' in this sense, is not the condition of the most intense competition possible but the freedom of the agents to adapt individually to the market processes and influence them. Such individual adaptations are the necessary requirement for market processes to function and to produce results. However, these adaptations can only come from the agents themselves.

Markets are therefore also learning processes or discovery procedures (see particularly Kirzner 1996 and also Mises 1927, 1949).

It is even possible that competition in general is the natural condition of market processes, (as Walrasian and Arrow-Debreu models, that is, institutional approaches with pre-set optima, or equilibria) would contend. But one cannot deduce therefore that a particular competition at a particular time is the natural or much less the ideal condition for a particular market – nor that this condition is *ex ante* identifiable. If markets are learning or discovery processes, their ideal condition is not known *ex ante* to the agents involved in these processes. Also, the different agents in the markets might have different learning processes, that is, even if the market is a process, the content of the process is different according to the individual agents. This axiomatically implies that the ideal condition of a market at any given time cannot be known to regulation or the regulators because it does not exist. Would this condition exist and would it be known *ex ante*, there would be no need for a market, and the achievement of any condition could more efficiently be left to central planning.

One possible riposte to these arguments could be that even if the regulator does not know the ideal condition at any time, the regulator can know that condition 'x' is better than condition 'y.' There is even a more prosaic way of stating this argument; the carpenter cannot make an ideal table, but she can make a pretty good table. This type of argument has, however, two fallacies. The first one is easy to spot. The carpenter lives in a world of actual or possible competition. So, even if no carpenter can make the ideal table, customers can refrain from engaging in exchange with those carpenters that make subpar tables. The case with competition regulation is different. Objects of that regulation cannot just look for another regulator. While there is a disciplinary effect of market processes on carpenters and other participants of these processes, there is none on competition regulators. Therefore, their judgement of condition 'x' being better than condition 'y' is not accessible by those for whom they are making the decision. Ironically, the regulation of competition is a monopoly of the regulator. The second way in which the argument fails will be dealt with more in the discussion of the overtaxation made by competition regulation. It suffices to say that the judgement is highly dependent on static models that are based on an ideal or natural state of the market and have a tendency not to incorporate the different value judgements by the agents of markets. Stating that the market condition 'x' is better than 'y' entails a claim on the end-state of a given market. So here again, why are markets as processes even necessary?

In sum, competition regulation overtaxes its idea of markets because it is too attached to an institutional view of markets and presupposes that some instance – the regulator, at any rate – knows more about the market than the market itself; thus making the market obsolete as an instrument. Instead, competition regulation dismisses the open-ended, undetermined nature of market processes.

But competition regulation is also overtaxing itself, for the institutional model of markets it relies on cannot deliver what it promises. It is commonly said that the competition regulation's goal is to increase consumer welfare, increase social welfare and increase competition efficiency (paradigmatic in Motta 2004, pp. 17ff.). Note that there is a deeper issue about what welfare is or entails. Economic welfare is a general concept that does not lend to easy definition. Basically, it refers to how well people are doing. Economic welfare is usually measured in terms of real income or real gross domestic product (GDP). This measurement suggests that people are better off and therefore there is an increase in economic welfare, whenever a higher real income or higher GDP is achieved. However, economic welfare will be concerned with more than just levels of income. For example, people's living standards are also influenced by factors such as levels of congestion and pollution. These quality of life factors are important in determining economic welfare.[7]

If it is the aim of competition regulation to increase the overall welfare of a society, then competition regulators would need direct and exclusive access to a large stock of information. The problem of welfare maximization is closely related to the omniscience discussed above but nuanced a bit differently. Above, it was shown that competition regulation as such needs to know more about the market than the market knows. The problem with welfare is that the engineer of welfare must also know more about each individual agent than the agents themselves. The engineer of welfare would exclusively need to know all preferences of all agents or groups of agents at any given time in the market process in order to calculate the general welfare. Buchanan (1959, p. 126) formulates it like this:

> Welfare economists, new and old have generally assumed omniscience in the observer, although this assumption is rarely made explicit, and even more rarely are its implications examined. The observing economist is considered to be able to 'read' individual preference functions. Thus, even though an 'increase in welfare' for an individual is defined as 'movement to a preferred position,' the economist can unambiguously distinguish an increase in welfare independent of individual behavior because he can accurately predict what the

individual would, in fact, 'choose' if confronted with the alternatives under consideration.

If markets are understood as processes, neither the regulator nor the welfare economist à la Buchanan could know enough, since individual decisions are not entirely foreseeable or predictable. The outcome of the market, that is, of each individual exchange, does not occur because of covering laws, but they are unique tokens of different decisions that cannot be completely reconstructed *post facto*, let alone be predicted *ex ante*. Buchanan (1959, p. 126) stresses this point:

> The omniscience assumption seems wholly unacceptable. Utility is measurable, ordinally or cardinally, only to the individual decision-maker. It is a subjectively quantifiable magnitude. While the economist may be able to make certain presumptions about 'utility' on the basis of observed facts about behavior, he must remain fundamentally ignorant concerning the actual ranking of alternatives until and unless that ranking is revealed by the overt action of the individual choosing.

Imagine that an individual agent decides not to engage in a certain market exchange. Competition regulation thus demands of itself not only to know more than the agents that engage in exchange but also those agents who have decided not to participate in a particular market. This decision takes place in the form of the consumption of substitutes or in non-consumption. Markets disclose information about the preferences and actions of the agents in market processes – but when several agents do not participate in a particular market, this information is missing because it is perhaps non-existent. Regardless of this, competition regulation expects knowledge about the non-existent from the regulator, that is, competition regulation is bound to know all possible epistemic states (which is highly unlikely but logically conceivable) and all non-existing epistemic states (which is logically inadmissible; one cannot know the unknown).

What is more, under the maxim of social welfare, competition regulation has to develop, anticipate and judge common social conditions. At this point, there is another overstrain: the welfare of the buyers quite often stands in direct contradiction with social welfare in general. How to judge what is best for the overall system? How to judge it in a capitalistic system, in which a large number of the buyers are also owners of the enterprises that cause alleged inefficiencies in perfect competition? Not to forget that the state assumes the right to induce distortions of competition in the name of social welfare; how to differentiate state-induced distortions from other alleged distortions? How to separate state-tolerated distortions from others?

Unless the relevant choices are to be made by some entity other than individual themselves, why is there any need to construct a 'social' value scale? There would seem to be no reason for making interpersonal comparisons of 'welfare' based on hypothetical individual preferences except for the purpose of assisting in the attainment of given ends for the group or some subgroup. This central feature of the approach seems, therefore, to be contrary to one of the presuppositions of the free society. The function may be useful as a device in assisting the decision-making of a despot, benevolent or otherwise, an organic state, or a single-minded ruling group. (Buchanan 1959, p. 133)

In other words, competition regulation also makes excessive demands on itself because it not only has to take care of competition but also of social and individual welfare, which themselves are to be judged outside the categories of competition – and therefore out of the reach of competition regulation. Competition regulation is detrimental to the view of markets as a series of exchanges between individuals or group. To the contrary, competition regulation serves to institute presupposed end-states; presupposed by a central ruling body.

Here, another challenge arises: it not only has a wrong understanding of the individuals' actions and of the market but it also has shortcomings within its own economic theory. Competition regulation has its basis in welfare economics, which is oriented toward the so-called Pareto criteria in welfare economics. They are: an optimum is reached when no individual can be benefited without adversely affecting another; and if a state of affairs allows benefiting an individual without affecting adversely another, the individual should be benefited (see, for example, Reetz 2005). While the first principle is descriptive in nature (although descriptive on a normatively bound position), the second is prescriptive. In the context of competition regulation, the regulator has to institute a system of 'perfect competition' in which individuals are benefited to the optimum. This entails two steps. The first is decomposing any elements of imperfect competition and the second is the reallocation of outcomes. While earlier this idea was criticized for not being compatible with free markets, the same idea also has problems within its own economic theory.

First, it is static, which seems to presuppose that each market has one point of equilibrium, or one optimum. This is consistent with Arrow-Debreu/Walrasian economics on which it is grounded and that relies on the general equilibria of markets. But it also seems to presuppose that once this equilibrium is found, it does not change. This is not consistent with models of general equilibria since they allow for dynamic changes in the exact outcome of equilibria. At worst, competition regulation entails the general halt of all market exchanges once the optimal equilibrium in found; at best, regulators are chasing after optimum welfare and since it changes, they will be continuously intervening in the markets; but not because of the markets but because of their chase. Second, it assumes a constant marginal rate of (factor) substitution (also intertemporal), and the same marginal productivity of all factors (also intertemporal). These assumptions are just simplifications of the market model that do not yield a theoretical basis. If all production factors were to have the same marginal productivity, there would be no need for differentiation among them; also, other branches of economics that rely on equilibria, like labor economics and the theory of capital, would have no object of study at all, since they study the specific composite of labor or capital and how to increase their productivity as well as their differentiation. Third, the model of competition regulation relies exclusively on perfect competition.

The problem with the last two: the ideal of perfect competition, like the theorem of constant factor substitution (principle of homogeneity), is part of the microeconomic theory of market equilibrium. More precisely, it encompasses those preconditions that allow the development of a single equilibrium in the market (Arrow and Hahn 1971). As well known as both assumptions are, their application is limited to the introductory theory of economics; few economists would accept the effectiveness of these assumptions uncritically in the real economy. In short, they are textbook simplifications and lack a theoretical ground in themselves. Some might object now that some markets, at least financial markets, show a remarkable resemblance to the model. Apart from boom-and-bust cycles, data corroborate this objection. Financial markets have a 'natural' tendency toward equilibria. The question is, then, why so? In the financial markets, agents, be they institution or individuals or even computer programing, act according to models. These models are derived from general equilibria models that themselves rely on the equilibrium, substitution and atomism assumptions discussed above. The general model of equilibrium generates a series of other models that are used in financial markets; therefore, it is the general model of equilibrium that creates the reality of financial markets. In other words, financial markets are autopoietic systems based on these principles (Brodbeck 1991). Real markets in the sense of markets for goods and services other than financial do not adjust their actions and exchanges to models; on the contrary, models are developed to explain the workings of real markets.

Note, however, that the word 'real' is not being used in order to dismiss or denigrate financial markets. 'Real' is the linguistic marker pointing at markets other than financial markets. More precisely, 'real' points at markets as understood by this book, that is, as a series of exchanges and process of gathering information, learning and adjusting by individuals or groups of individuals. Financial markets, in the meaning above, are those markets primarily dependent on models.

For the real markets, the assumptions that make it possible for market models to explain them and construct much of the realities in financial markets fall short. First, there will be transaction costs to enter into competitive, commercial or legal relationships, but also to terminate any such. Second, there will be further costs when production factors are exchanged. The respective costs will have a less potent effect if they can be redistributed to a larger structure; the larger the basis of cost allocation, the smaller the average cost rate. In other words, large enterprises can better distribute these additional costs to their structures, and by means of this absorption they more closely approach the principle of homogeneity. Small- and medium-sized enterprises (SMEs) cannot manage the same. This makes it quite clear that any regulation that does not consider the costs of transaction or assumes them equal to zero is simultaneously causing a structural distortion of the market in favor of some players (see Amstutz and Reinert 2004; Williamson 1979).

The hypothesis of perfect competition is based on the fact that market players carry neither transaction nor substitution costs. But these costs actually emerge, and for the sake of minimizing them, market players – suppliers and buyers – can unite in corporations, for instance, in the form of buying cooperatives, sales groups, vertical structures and so on. In order to approach the principle of homogeneity and thereby enjoy the advantages of economic cost reductions (which will be manifested in lower prices), the market players selectively give up perfect competition without abandoning it altogether as an option. Competition is a condition that allows collaboration and disciplines it by making it unilaterally callable at any time.

The understanding of the market, hidden behind competition regulation, neither corresponds with the understanding of markets as processes nor is adapted to the real economy. Just as there will be transaction costs (which are assumed to equal zero), the cooperation between competitors (suppliers and buyers) can lead to the reduction of market prices because general expenses (especially transaction costs) are spread to structures that absorb these costs and consequently lower them. Competition regulation, by contrast, takes the view that in a world without transaction costs, every cooperation benefits insiders in comparison to outsiders. But this is the wrong conclusion, based on the wrong assumptions.

Furthermore, even if the theoretical models consulted were 'consistent,' they are still being reduced in an undue manner by monitoring competition merely on the basis of prices (and in fewer cases on the basis of quantity), while the different facets of competition altogether, as well as their mutual complementation and their effects, remain theoretically and practically disregarded. There is competition between prices, locations, qualities, levels of service, brands, and competition within brands, between risks, information and its assessors, among others.

This second shortcoming of competition regulation is of a theoretical nature. Welfare is not an apt premise to work on. It has several problems as a theory per se and even if its premise is accepted, its theoretical development faces several issues of consistency. Also, relating this theory to the reality of markets proves difficult.

4.2.2　Problems with Institutions

Competition regulation has a problem with the model of markets and the competition it relies upon. But it also has a problem with its own institutional setting. Regulators – as institutions and individuals – regulate markets: they intervene in markets and thus influence market conditions as well as market results. In the course of the following paragraphs, it can be safely assumed that they are governed by the above-mentioned goals, like establishing an as-perfect-as-possible competition and maximizing welfare. It is the goals themselves that lay the foundation for the excess demands on the regulator. Not only does the regulator have to make use of models that do not do justice (as mentioned above) to market reality, but also tasks are imposed on him, which are epistemically impossible for him to master. This is revealed in at least three contexts.

First, the regulator must decide on the cases he has to or wishes to pursue, that is, from a variety of potential cases, he selects several, which he will then subject to his analysis and intervention. These cases may be brought to his attention from the outside, but the regulator must also act on his own initiative. Of course, there will be enough relevant information in reality, and on the grounds of institutional economics alone, a regulator will endeavor to spot as many indications as possible. This, however, requires that the regulator either knows the conditions of all possible markets or that he is in a position to analyse all markets and to recognize their respective conditions. Even if one can generously concede the former, the latter is more difficult in a logical sense. From an epistemic viewpoint, the regulator must closely approximate the market's state of knowledge in order to know the conditions of all markets, which means no less than that the regulator must asymptotically approximate the number of market players in his natural resources. If practice now argues that the regulator's focus is on the most important cases, this is an indirect admission that the regulator cannot achieve the goals imposed on him because he does not increase social welfare as something aggregate but rather the individual welfare of players in submarkets. Why should the market for hand cream be higher-ranking than the market for peanuts? It is in the implementation of competition regulation that competition authority is met with excessive demands.

Second, the challenge for the regulator is no less taxing if he focuses on one case alone. To know a market, its communication processes must be understood and shared in (in the sense of cost and benefits). From a third party perspective, markets can be characterized, but hardly known or understood. The regulator cannot participate in every market – this would distort the market he wishes to investigate. In order to evade this problem, he turns to a methodological approach: phenotypic market analysis. Different markets, each functioning differently and each by description a model in itself, are subsumed under even more abstract constructs. Similarities in structure and function have been postulated for the different already abstracted market descriptions. This makes it no longer necessary to understand the market for telephony as such because, in the abstract, it can be treated and judged equally as the market for sprouts. Because the market models for telephony and for sprouts have the same structure, it is assumed that the markets will function alike in reality – and that their respective ideal conditions can be determined in this abstraction. But: the market for taxicab companies is different from financial markets; the one for household appliances is different from the electricity market.

In the cases that competition regulators must or wish to act, they use abstract models; but they also need to match the abstract models with the economic reality of the cases, so they resort to analysing the specific markets gaining as much information as possible on them – in fact, in practice they gain so much information that it not only makes subsumption under the abstract model difficult in itself but information contradicting the subsumption is not sufficiently considered. This self-fulfilling logic even creates the epistemic illusion of having identified the 'right' market, of understanding it, being able to anticipate its ideal condition and initiate the necessary corrections. In reality though, this represents the transfer of a second-order model to a reality with doubtful empirical evidence. Martenet and Heinemann (2012) are a good example for this kind of excess demand. After initially admitting that the market is not an organizing principle (but rather the model of competition), they explicitly state that complete verification of an offense against competition as an organizing principle cannot be required from the regulator, but must take place with the necessary 'flexibility.'

The third problem of excessive demand on competition authority is of a practical nature. It is interesting to observe that any competition authority is committed to competition, because it brings to light alleged efficiencies – while, itself, it is equipped with absolute regional, quantity and price monopolies. Competition authorities are monopolists themselves. If it is true that players are only efficient in competition, the deduction must be that the one competition authority is necessarily inefficient (see Schneider 2013). This third problem altogether might prove damaging in two aspects. First, it might lead competition regulation to be overly protective of established models because these are the models regulators are anchored to. They know how the markets and the models based upon these markets work. This leads to regulators protecting the status quo (or even, vested interests) against novelties. Second, it might lead to competition regulators wanting to expand their regulatory power. This does not entail bad faith; on the contrary, the agent that understands itself as a maximizer of the general welfare will have an interest in really maximizing it. In order to achieve this goal, this agent will want to regulate all possible market interactions in order to maximize welfare.

But here again, the dilemma shows itself: if there is a need for a central regulator in order to maximize welfare, then why is there a need for anything but the regulator? Why are there markets and regulator? If the regulator is able by itself to maximize general welfare, then the market as such is not needed; needed are just its outcomes but these can be established beforehand by the regulator.

4.3 THE CASE OF UBER: DOES UBER CHANGE BECAUSE OF REGULATION?

This chapter is about the economics of regulation. The starting point were those taxicab companies protesting against Uber and claiming that its business model was one of unfair competition. Their so-called pro-competitive stance was that competition was fine as long as all agents are equally regulated. After a closer review of these so-called 'pro-competitive' arguments they were revealed to be, in fact, anti-competitive. Then, the perspective shifted toward competition regulation. It turns out that competition regulation itself diminishes competition by curbing the dynamics in the market processes. These insights will now be applied to Uber by responding to two questions. Is regulation curbing innovation? And does Uber respond to regulation by becoming less innovative?

4.3.1   Regulating Innovation

Not all regulation has negative side effects on innovation. There are laws facilitating private education, pushing research, lowering the tax and administrative burden on companies, giving them more free space, for example, in order to innovate. Some Austrian economists accept some types of regulation as necessary for the development of a free and innovative society. Among these regulations are principles like the basic right to life, property or opinion; among them are the procedural rules of due legal process, the rule of law in which the same law has the same validity to all its subjects, security and even some argue for intellectual property rights. How to reconcile this acceptance of some laws with insight that the more fine-grained regulation, the worse its effects on market processes?

First, let the question be properly set. Instead of claiming that all regulation is detrimental to innovation, lets state that regulation that directly intervenes in the market processes is generally in opposition to innovation. What is regulation that directly intervenes in the markets? Roughly, different types of regulation can be differentiated. First of all, there are basic rights, like the aforementioned rights to life, property or opinion and expression. Then, there are procedural rights, like how to address a judge or a jury, what the police can do, which actions a person has to take in order to home educate children or which forms to fill in when applying for a visa. Regulation that directly intervenes in the markets is mainly concerned with the actions of individuals and groups as they engage in exchanges of goods, services and information. Of course, some of the other regulations also influence the market, for example, having to fill out a visa form diminishes my ability to engage in the market process in a foreign country. But visa forms are not primarily about markets. Vice versa, market regulations might affect other areas, for example, real estate statutes influence the limits of property rights, but real estate statutes were not primarily conceived because of property rights or in order to influence them, they were implemented for regulating the real estate market.

A simple objection might arise now: there is no regulation primarily concerned with the markets because all regulations influence many other different regulatory realms. This is the case because regulation is part of a holistic system. This objection misses two points. First, if everything were to be governed by a holistic regulation, then the specific regulation of markets would not be needed. Its very existence is an indicator of its *sui generis* necessity. Second, all rules have this sort of normative openness. This is characteristic of all legal systems (see Hart 1961) because legal systems and rules, like much of human reality, are shaped by language and language has an open texture (see Wittgenstein 1945 and especially Searle 1995 for social reality and 'objects').

As much as regulation can be tied to a system of interdependences, it is, in practice, possible to identify those specific regulations that have a market at the center of their attention and those that do not. Even those regulations that regulate among other things market behavior can be counted to the group being treated here. It is not the idea now to create a list of regulations dealing with markets and their agents; it suffices to say that they are in principle recognizable as such. In this book, at least two different types have been studied as examples: sectorial regulations defining standards, licenses and the like; and competition regulation.

So, it is argued here that the specific regulation of market agents or single markets has detrimental effects on innovation. This does not mean that these effects are not to be mitigated by the market; in fact, they are because market agents start to factor these effects into their preferences and actions. But instead of increasing the efficiency or the freedom of the markets, these regulations decrease them. If innovation occurs, then it is in spite of and never aided by this type of regulation.

Which are the mechanisms that cause this opposition? Recalling the conception of innovation used here, it can take several forms. It can occur as a new technology, a new good, a new service, different marketing, different production structure, different organization of the form or even a different legal set-up. It is in the nature of innovation to be unpredictable in which form and with which content it will materialize. Regulation of single markets and sectors, and regulation of competition rely on knowing its objects and predicting how they act. Knowing the objects of regulation entails having a clear conception of what they are, how they are traded or exchanged, how information on them can be gathered by the agents of a market. Predicting the agents' actions means being in principle able to discern some patterns of their behavior and stipulate that these patterns will repeat themselves in the future. Both knowing the object of regulation and predicting the agents' actions is done by applying regulatory standards and models.

These standards and models, however, can only capture what is already known. Innovation by its very definition cannot be known before its materialization. This dilemma has two types of detrimental effects on innovation. The first option is firms accepting the regulatory framework and even if they develop new ideas they will try to develop them within the scope of the given regulation. Look at the incumbent taxicab providers – they developed apps to hail a cab, but just their own taxis and without the option of negotiating a price; also, they did not innovate on using spare capacity, their innovation was to expand capacity as needed. Of course, there are innovations, but to a much lesser degree than what would be possible. And that is one detrimental effect of market regulation on innovation. By subjecting all agents to standards and models, agents have no incentives to innovate outside the standards and models, even if that type of innovation would bring them more benefits. Also, since regulation guarantees advantages for the regulated companies, they have less incentives to innovate, they seek to maintain and maximize their surplus rents that emanate from regulation. Instead of pursuing benefits in the market, possible at the cost of other firms, these regulated companies are happy to pursue their benefits in regulation at the cost of all other agents, especially consumers (by depriving them of the benefits of innovation, be these lower prices, higher quality, faster service, etc.).

The second detrimental effect is when firms that innovate outside the regulatory framework are brought into it as they release their regulation. Once again, look at the taxicab industry. Uber's innovation would make it possible that every spare or unused car capacity could be marketed as a service of transportation. By applying regulation on Uber, this idea was de facto abandoned and only licensed drivers or even licensed taxicabs are able to market their services. By bringing Uber inside the regulatory realm, the scope of its innovation was considerably reduced. One could even say, by bringing Uber within the regulatory realm, the innovator became just another taxicab company. This problem is summed up by McCraw (2006) who opposes Keynes's approach, which is pro-regulation, over Schumpeter's, which is pro-innovation:

> Throughout The General Theory, Keynes 'pleads for a definite policy and on every page the ghost of that policy looks over the shoulder of the analyst, frames his assumptions, guides his pen.' Overall, says Schumpeter, 'the capitalist process is essentially a process of change of the type which is being assumed away in this book.' In Keynesian and other macroeconomic models, individual entrepreneurs, companies, and industries vanish from the scene. (p. 236)

What does this all mean for the taxicab industry being studied here? True pro-innovation (and pro-competitive) forces in the taxi industry would take the advent of Uber as a token for the possibility of successfully providing taxi services of quality outside the regulatory framework. Therefore, they would demand the simplification of the regulation or even its abolition altogether.

4.3.2 Changing Uber

In Chapter 2, Uber's business model at the time of its launch was explained. The idea: if anyone had spare capacity and wanted to make money with those free seats in the car, one could offer on the app and customers willing to take a ride in a stranger's car could hail it through the same app. Uber was nothing more than the technology platform that intermediated supply and demand. As the firm started to grow, Uber started to give more directives to the drivers offering their services on the platform. These directives were about pricing, service, quality and even 'corporate identity.' These changes to the model were not regulation-driven. They were growth-driven. As the technology platform grew, it wanted to be perceived as a brand of service by the market. That might be usual, but it also calls the self-description of Uber as a mere technology platform into question.

From its own business perspective, it is natural for Uber to brand itself and extend that brand through a series of directives to all its partners. After all, a startup needs financing. And the better the brand is established, the more attractive the startup becomes to investors. Also, the more recognizable the product or service, the clearer it becomes a brand. The aim here is not to discuss how Uber changed because of its intrinsic growth-related aims, but how it changed its products because of regulation. Naturally, it is difficult to isolate single drivers of change, but there are some developments that would not have happened in the absence of regulatory pressure. The materials for this subsection were collected from Uber's own business model (portrayed through its website in different versions in the United States and Europe) (see Edelman and Geradin 2015; McBride 2015; Rauch and Schleicher 2015).

But now Uber is changing. In six years, Uber built up a market base and reached a certain standing. But more importantly, Uber learned a lot. It learned about itself and adjusted to it. Uber introduced different service levels, quality control, different forms of cooperation with the drivers, ways of using consumer data and so on. Uber learned the dynamic process of the market on how to deal with itself. And Uber also learned how to deal with the markets. It adapted different product lines to different markets, it found out how to deal with traditional taxicabs and it learned how to adapt to regulation. And this is one of the outcomes of the market process. And in this 'Austrian' verve, it is a potentially problematic one, because Uber learned not only to take advantage of its own entrepreneurship, but also of regulation.

Uber is diversifying and changing its strategy. After having fought different legal issues, especially in the years 2013 and 2014, it changed parts of its business model. The most important changes to its business model were made in Europe, but they are also being implemented in the United States, albeit at a slower pace. In some countries like France and Germany, Uber hints at accepting being treated as a taxi company: it insures its cars and drivers, it applies for licenses or medallions and it even owns cars. The question is not about the merits of this change but about how the change and regulation interact. Here are some examples.

The first example is UberPOP. Drivers only charge for the costs of transportation to the clients. This means the drivers cannot make any profits from transporting people. Uber pays the drivers a surplus in order to compensate for profits. The move eliminates driver profits, which allows them to offer rides without a license under local law. From the law's perspective, UberPOP is basically a car-sharing service and not a taxi-like transportation. The unlicensed drivers still have the incentive to offer their services since Uber is paying them a premium to do so and taking care of insurance. How this is to be seen by law enforcers still remains unclear; France decided to ban it, Germany accepts it. Either way, it is clear that Uber changed its business model because of regulation when introducing UberPOP. First, the technology platform is doing much more than allocating free capacity; it is paying fixed costs of the supply side's, that is, drivers, and paying them to offer their services. Uber would not have done so if the drivers were allowed to run unlicensed capacity-sharing services on their own. And second, Uber is taking responsibility vis-à-vis regulators for its drivers. This becomes apparent in its launching of UberPOP and telling 'its' drivers how to run their business. A 'mere' technology platform would not do that, indeed it would not take responsibility for the regulatory problem. However, Uber, in doing so, and by reacting to regulatory pressure, shows that it understands its business not only as a technology provider, but also as an actual transportation provider. Again, the claim is not that Uber changed its view on its own business because of regulation, but that regulation propelled development in Uber, and that some of these changes also modified the very idea of its own operation.

The second example is UberPOOL, which was introduced in 2014 in San Francisco, New York and Paris (just a month after a French court had deemed the company's UberPOP service to be illegal). UberPOOL matches a rider with another rider who is travelling in the same direction. If a match cannot be found, riders are offered a discount on a regular Uber trip – in the United States only. The regulatory impact on such a service is less evident. But it is still there. As Uber admitted, UberPOOL is the next iteration of UberPOP because it is more about sharing than it is about offering a taxi-like transportation. If competing with taxis had been easier, it is less probable that Uber would start to explore the ride-sharing at no or less profit. Also, it would be considerably less probable that Uber would be willing to cannibalize the taxi-like services it offers by granting a discount on the taxi service if a customer does not find a match in the UberPOOL concept. By introducing UberPOOL and its integration with the classic Uber service, Uber as a company is showing once again that it is not just a technology platform, but also a transportation company. And again, whereas it is not solely a function of regulation that these changes come, it is through regulation that their dynamism occurs at a faster pace.

The third example is UberBLACK, a limousine operation. Uber-BLACK cars are a more upscale service, but they rely on registered cars and licensed drivers. The step makes UberBLACK more closely resemble a traditional taxi operation. In some places of operation, especially in Europe, Uber is the entity buying the limousines. This represents a noticeable change in the company's business model, since it transforms the facilitation of unused capacity exchange to capacity provider. Here, the influence of regulation becomes the most transparent: Uber simply accepts regulation to its fullest consequence and mutates from technology provider and/or matchmaker to, basically, a taxi company.

UberX serves as the fourth example. These are licensed cars. They might not be licensed as cab drivers with the iconic New Yorker medallion, but they are licensed. In this case, Uber submitted to regulation. As in this whole chapter and book, this is not a normative claim but an empirical one. By submitting to regulation, Uber explicitly acknowledges the change in its original business model: it transitioned from technology platform to a transportation company. It is worth noting that in some – European – jurisdictions, Uber registered its UberX services as a rent-a-car. This shows that the company is trying to arbitrage regulation. Arbitrage is the practice of taking advantage of differences in two separate regulations for what can be considered the same product – at least from the customers' point of view.

There are more examples of changes either induced or accelerated by regulation in the Uber universe. However, there are also expansions of the business model that have nothing to do with regulation – at least, not at first sight. One example is UberFRESH, a lunch delivery service, in Santa Monica, and the other example is UberCARGO, a van rental service, in Hong Kong. A company expanding its business model is natural. But would a 'pure' technology provider serve you lunch? And what is the reason for offering logistics services in Hong Kong? Simple: the van rental market in the city-state is not regulated – but the taxi market is (Guo and Tang 2015). It is not argued here that Uber is diversifying because of regulation. But it is a valid point that, since regulation makes further advancement in the initial area of operation more difficult and more expensive, it is natural for Uber to seek expansion in less regulated and thus less difficult areas of operation. This, however, changes the nature of the firm that started as a technology provider. With the addition of these last two examples to its business, Uber morphed from a technology platform via a transportation company to a full-blown provider of logistics services.

These are just some examples of how regulation changes or accelerates changes in Uber's business model. There are other ways in which regulation can impact Uber too. Without resulting in an immediate adaptation of the business model, regulation can influence the organization of Uber's resources. One example is California's Labor Commission, ruling that at least one Uber driver is an employee. As it stands now, Uber employs its drivers as third party contractors, operating as a logistics company that provides access to customer demand and directions, transactions and so on for the drivers. Uber has argued repeatedly in various courts that it is not a transportation or taxi company, but rather a software platform that matches customer demand with supply. This ruling changes that, turning Uber into a transportation startup instead of a logistics software company. That puts the company in a position to face a number of legal obstacles, as well as rising costs of employing those drivers directly and offering them benefits and so on. It remains to be seen how this will affect Uber's organization and, then again, its business model.

Is this problematic? Not per se. It is normal that Uber learns and adapts. But it might not be what regulation wanted. Regulation and its proponents wanted to transform Uber into a traditional taxicab company. Instead, Uber transformed itself into a much broader and deeper provider of logistics. From the point of view of those that institutionally wanted to reach an optimum or to institutionally create conditions for the market of taxicab reaching equilibrium, the plan did not work. Uber legally circumvented regulation by innovating itself. 'Austrian' economists, however, would have worried for another, equally possible case: Uber is not only adhering to regulation, it is also 'capturing' it, influencing it to drive other taxicabs out of business. But this is a discussion for the conclusion.

SUMMARY

Are innovation and regulation opposites? From a perspective that understands markets as open-ended, undeterminate processes, regulation is detrimental to innovation. Regulation presupposes a certain idea of the results of the markets. Often, this is not made explicit in the regulation itself, but being willing to make rules implies not being willing to accept any behavior or outcome. This chapter has also explained how regulation serves the status quo by using the status quo to measure innovation. By necessity, innovation is different from the actual state of affairs, and, insofar as actual regulation is used to measure it, deviant. Actual regulation, by 'correcting' the deviances of innovation diminishes the innovative content or brings the whole process to a halt. So, to answer the leading question of the chapter: yes, innovation and regulation are opposites.

Is Uber changing its business model because of regulation? Using the example of Uber, it has been shown how the company adapts to regulation and how, in adapting to it, it changes its own business model and diversifies it into less regulated realms. Instead of advancing innovation in the markets it started to 'disrupt,' Uber opts for complying and diminishes the development of new technology or products that were able to revolutionize these markets. Instead it expands to more generic, that is, less innovative, products.

NOTES

1. Contrary to common belief, chaos does not denote the absence of any order. Although in everyday language 'chaos' often carries a negative connotation, in its scientific use, it is value neutral. Usually, chaotic systems have (extreme) sensitivity to initial conditions, their cause-and-effect relations are not proportional and they are non-linear (Smith 1998).
2. On a normative note, this author would strongly disagree.
3. Arbitrage usually denotes the simultaneous purchase and sale of an asset in order to profit from a difference in the price. Regulatory arbitrage extends this principle to denote the practice of legally circumventing regulation, for example, by finding loopholes or influencing regulation for particular ends.
4. This section discusses two arguments put forward by so-called pro-competition advocates. Both have shown to be, in reality, anti-competitive. There is yet another form of competition regulation not discussed in this book: minimum wages. For the (mostly negative) implications of the minimum wage, refer to Hovenga et al. (2013) and Diamond (2014).
5. In the United States, the focus of competition regulation is anti-trust. This has, for one, historical roots, but also shows a greater adaptability to market processes. While the foremost problem in the United States is how to prevent single agents from dominating the market processes, in Europe the primary concern is how to prevent agents from cooperating and through cooperative behavior form cartels.
6. Perfect competition, in the institutional view of markets, is the condition of the market when the following criteria are met: first, all suppliers offer the same product; second, all suppliers are price takers – they cannot control the market price of their product; third, all suppliers have a relatively small market share; fourth, buyers have complete information about the product being sold and the prices charged by each supplier; and fifth, the industry is characterized by freedom of entry and exit (Motta 2004).

7. This does not mean that the measurement must or should be changed. Quite the contrary, the measurement is fine. The problem is reducing economic contexts to simple cause-and-effects relations. And the even more pressing problem is to reduce policy or regulation to simple cause-and-effects relations, for example, by fixing them on only one measurement.

Conclusion: destroying Uber, the destroyer?

The original Uber strategy made Uber an agent of creative destruction. It intermediates idle transportation capacity through network effects and technology. With a novel product geared at an attractive lifestyle, noisy marketing and the specific targeting of celebrities and hipsters, Uber started what could be a disruption of the taxi industry. This agent of creative destruction, however, was soon to face several adversities.

In a world consisting of anything but the preferences and actions of individuals and groups of individuals, the innovator faces only three adversities: (1) its own ability to maintain its innovation, (2) the response of the demand side of the market processes to the novelty and (3) the response by the other agents in the supply side of the market processes to the innovation, whereby this last response is even more innovative than the innovator.

However, the real world consists of many other agents than those engaged in spontaneous exchange. The world also consists of regulations and regulatory bodies. In the reality of regulated markets, there is an additional adversity: legal actions. These are not fruits of the market as a process of individual revelation of preferences but an agent outside the market. But this outside agent can be more powerful than the market processes themselves because it claims a privilege over the market exchange process. Uber's competitors were quick to call this outside agent to action. Their call was to the regulatory agent to regulate Uber, even at the cost of diminishing, or even halting, its disruptive effects. Indeed, many competitors secretly hoped that the regulatory agents would not only see halting Uber's innovation as a cost of their regulative action but as the very aim of it. And so Uber, the innovator, was forced to deal with regulatory response.

The question the future poses is: what happens if Uber submits to regulation and starts to play the regulatory game? It has been established that the inner logic of regulation has detrimental effects on innovation and on the market processes as a way of spontaneous exchange, at least in the realm of the regulation of the taxi industry. Also, it has been established that Uber accepts regulation, albeit reluctantly, and changes its business model in order to adapt to it. By doing so, it is also becoming less innovative. For example, instead of taking free allocation of capacity to the next level – be it including more plug-and-play drivers or concentrating on free auctioning of other excess capacity like mobile broadband – Uber decided to expand to other areas in which regulatory burden is less, for example, serving lunch. In these new areas, Uber is not innovating; it is just copying business models that already exist.

Uber is losing its innovative edge. From the rational perspective of a company trying not only to succeed in the markets, but also to legitimize the investments that have been made and to make some profit, the firm is right in establishing profits in those areas in which marginal costs of operations are lower. Logically, Uber is opting for success through expansion rather than success through innovation. There are no regulatory limits to getting bigger, so far. Perhaps Uber is trying to become too big to ban.

So, Uber has different ways to play regulation. First, it can abide by it, change its services and even its business model to comply. Many examples for this were quoted in Chapter 3. Second, Uber could try to navigate regulation in pursuit of regulatory arbitrage. One example is trying to operate services under a car rental instead of taxi regulation. Third, it can try to become too big to ban or too ingrained in the local distribution networks in those jurisdictions where it faces the danger of being banned. Fourth, if it is a political power or too big a company, Uber could use this advantage to influence regulation itself.

Before turning to this last point in more detail, let it be emphasized that all these four ways of dealing with regulation are rational from the individual firm's perspective. After all, each company has to find a way to deal with the regulatory overhead. But at the same time, none of these tactics advance innovation. By concentrating in playing regulation, Uber neglects the driver of its former success; innovation. Keeping this in mind, the last tactic mentioned above deserves closer scrutiny.

It has been said that the fourth option Uber has when dealing with regulation is to directly influence it. This presupposes a position of some strength. About 50 US jurisdictions have adopted ordinances recognizing Uber as a new type of transit provider called 'transportation network companies.' Each government, whether municipal or state, goes through its own process to craft rules, but in the end, officials generally codify the insurance coverage, background check policies and inspection protocols Uber already has in place. This means that Uber makes the rules. Although Uber promotes itself as a great disrupter, it has quickly mastered the old art of political influence. Uber built one of the largest and most successful lobbying forces in the United States, with a presence in almost every statehouse. It has 250 lobbyists and 29 lobbying firms registered in state-wide and nationwide lobby cadasters.[1]

There is some irony in that even Uber has been rallying behind these so-called competitive arguments analysed in the third chapter of this book. Suddenly, Uber is making a case for a 'level playing field' and for 'sectorial quality.' Uber also accepted the idea of competition regulation. All this happened through lobbying.

Since becoming an insider, and especially since facing legal action and eventual bans, Uber has adhered to some regulation not just as a result of a free-willed concern about quality, but also to achieve the legitimacy that comes from being regulated, as long as it can compete with standard taxis solely in terms of quality and price. It is interesting to note how Uber's strategy is changing with time. At the beginning, as it was the disruptive force, Uber stood against all and any regulation, defying it. As it became an insider, it started to adopt insurance and other quality policies similar to the direct – regulated – competition. And, as it turns to be a major force in the market, it endorses full regulation. This leads back again to the first argument, to the 'level playing field.' As Uber becomes a major supply side agent in the markets, it starts to demand equal regulation for all. But since regulation is a political process and happens in dialogue with the industry, Uber invests in influencing regulators and regulation.

In 2015, the company also released two rosy, data-heavy reports about the service's advantages on cities, drivers and communities. And, in an uncommon display of humility, Uber pledged to strengthen its user data privacy practices, acknowledging that 'we haven't always gotten it right.'[2] In August 2014, the company hired David Plouffe, the longtime confidant of President Obama, as Uber's Senior Vice President for Policy and Strategy. Plouffe leaned heavily on data to aim messages at voters during Mr Obama's campaign, and has already begun to use much the same strategy at Uber.[3]

The case being made here does not address the moral quality of Uber's influencing regulation. After all, it has been argued that regulation is per se open to external influence. The more important case is that Uber, by dedicating resources to deal with and influence regulation, neglects innovation, its primary driver. This neglect is transferring in the loss of innovative power and the adding up of problems. Wired puts it like this:

> But the real peril to Uber isn't bad PR. It's the costs of recruiting drivers and what that says about Uber's business model compared to those of traditional software companies. More drivers don't equal more value added. They simply equal staying alive. To get, keep, and expand its roster of drivers, Uber must

sink money into marketing, operations, and insurance in a way that, say, Google or Facebook never had to. Such on-the-ground expenditures don't carry the obvious promise of an exponential return on investment. In tech, spending on product, R&D, and talent create what entrepreneurs and investors like to describe as asymmetrical leverage. Take Dropbox. The file-syncing startup only needed a few hundred employees and a few data centers to hit a multi-billion-dollar valuation. Uber needs that, plus an army of drivers in cars. (Uber says its 'generating 20,000 new driver jobs every month.') Though Uber is a tech company, its product doesn't make sense without the piece that inhabits the physical world. And the physical world is notoriously inefficient. In the brief history of online businesses, competitive advantage typically has been gained by virtualizing away the costs of the physical, or lost by failing to shed that real-world weight. Amazon used the web to eliminate the overhead of brick-and-mortar retail stores. Newspapers were weighed down by the costs of paper and ink. But Uber isn't really using tech to make something that was once physical virtual. It's simply taking an existing service – hailing and dispatching rides –and making it better by leveraging mobile tech to make it more efficient. The need for a physical operation on the ground doesn't shrink. On the contrary, Uber's physical footprint keeps growing. On Thursday, it announced its expansion into 24 more cities, bringing the worldwide total to 205 cities in 45 countries. Uber, as the company itself says, wants to be everywhere.[4]

Where does that leave Uber now? Uber was built upon the convergence of two ideas: the market for free capacity and the potential of every person with overcapacity to become part of the supply side of that market through an action model. The creative disruption it started was faced with opposition by the industry it had the potential to 'destroy' and by regulators, who, lacking a framework to assess the impacts of creative destruction on society, prefer to 'save' the structure of the status quo. Uber itself, as soon as it entered the industry, became part of it by choosing not to jeopardize its own position and instead to roll back the creative destruction it started. As Uber was a small startup, it used disruptive innovation to destroy the market. It challenged regulation, regulatory bodies and its competition. The more it grew and the more of an insider it became, the more Uber accepted regulation (because with scale it had the financial means to comply). Now that Uber itself is one of the major forces in the market, it is the one influencing regulation, so that the taxi market will become more like a market for Uber. With its financial means it might intend to squeeze other companies of the markets by demanding regulation that favors its own business model. This means that from an agent of creative disruption, Uber will become one of the deterrents of innovation. Since Uber became an established agent, it has ceased to be the innovative disruptor and started to curb the process of creative destruction it started. Regulation proved a good instrument for this.

This is not a normative claim. It lies within the rationality of Uber to do such. This change in strategy only further exemplifies the problems with regulation of markets discussed in Chapter 2. Uber is using regulation of a specific market in order to solidify its position in that market. Uber's strategic move just proves the point that regulation, even one masked by the 'level playing field' argument, produces winners and losers and Uber speculates that it will be a winner. Note also that Uber adapting its business model to regulation does not mean that it is not continuing to innovate. It can innovate within the realm of regulation. For example, it can continue to develop its pricing algorithm that is, itself, an innovation. From the point of view of other market agents, this might only seem a part of possible innovation, but for Uber it can be the one feature to concentrate on. As argued toward the end of Chapter 3, companies operating under the regulation of markets can continue to innovate, but not in the full spectrum, just in the one allowed by the regulatory framework.

The claim 'role is self' as advanced by the philosopher Henry Rosemont (2015) is a radical communitarian claim meaning that it is not the individual person who is the ontic, epistemic and pragmatic privilege, but the social network. Every single being exists only because of those social relationships in which it is tied. There is no individuality without or outside these social networks. The validity of this point of view will not be discussed here. However, the motto 'role is self' can easily be used in the analysis being employed here. If a company innovates and tries to challenge the markets, it takes the role of agent of creative destruction. Even if it does not state that it is about destruction, creativity or innovation, the role that it plays is all the markets know about it. Therefore, and independently from the self-description of the given company, its role is the one of destructor and the market, that is, the other agents engaged in exchange, regard it as such. If that firm changes its strategy and favors regulation, acts like an insider or even squeezes out other newcomers, it plays the role of incumbent agent with vested interests. And since that role is all the market processes know about this firm, it becomes what it is. Here again, Schumpeter might be right in his claim that no entrepreneur can only act as an entrepreneur all the time. Market agents change their role as a function of how much innovation they need and/or are prepared to advance. Sometimes, market agents are even prepared to stop and scale their own innovations back if they judge that their benefit will be diminished by innovating more. However, and as they do so, they change their role from innovator to incumbent. This also means that some other agent will take up the role of innovator and agent of creative destruction.

Uber destroyed some part of its own creative destruction. By doing so, it has become vulnerable to new innovative business models that will continue to appear based on the two ideas that marked Uber's ascent: the convergence of auctioning free capacity in the taxicab industry and real-time life auctioning of that capacity. In other words, by destroying creative destruction, Uber risks being destroyed itself.

This book has focused on creative destruction and disruptive innovation as a capitalistic process, or even a driving force of capitalism, free market processes and increased efficiency. It then introduced specific regulations and the idea of competition regulation as a counterforce curbing creative destruction and its consequences. Their colliding against each other often leads to a victory of regulation over creative destruction because even market agents feel compelled to rally behind regulation as a protection against creative destruction. Even the agents of disruption, as they become insiders, are willing to become regulated. There is, however, another development. As former creative destructors become insiders, they become the object of destruction themselves.

SUMMARY

Is someone destroying Uber, the destroyer? Many would like to. Sectorial and competition regulation could end in destroying the innovation of Uber, of the company. But there is also the danger of self-destruction: the more Uber adapts to regulation or submits to it, the less it innovates. This means that if Uber does not continue to disrupt the taxicab industry by innovating, it will itself become the target of even newer market entrants, even more disruptive innovators. By destroying creative destruction, Uber risks being destroyed itself.

NOTES

1. Bloomberg (2015), 'This is how Uber takes over a city,' accessed 29 May 2016 at http://www.bloomberg.com/news/features/2015-06-23/this-is-how-uber-takes-over-a-city.
2. New York Times (2015), 'Hard charging Uber tries olive branch,' accessed 29 May 2016 at http://www.nytimes.com/2015/02/02/business/hard-charging-uber-tries-olive-branch.html.
3. http://blog.uber.com/davidplouffe (accessed 27 December 2015).
4. Wired (2014), 'Uber's biggest danger is its business model, not bad PR,' 29 August, accessed 29 May 2016 at http://www.wired.com/2014/08/the-peril-to-uber-is-its-business-model-not-bad-pr/.

References

Akerlof , G. (1970), 'The market for lemons: quality uncertainty and the market mechanism', *Quarterly Journal of Economics*, **84** (3), 488–500.

Allen, R.C. (2009), *The British Industrial Revolution in Global Perspective*, Cambridge: Cambridge University Press.

Amstutz, M. and M. Reinert (2004), 'Vertikale Preis- und Gebietsabreden – Eine kritische Analyse von Art. 5 Abs. 4 KG', *Jusletter*, accessed 29 May 2016 at http://www.baerkarrer.ch/publications/03_Amstutz_Reinert.pdf.

Anderson, W. (2001), 'Lemons and the Nobel Prize', Mises Institute, accessed 29 May 2016 at http://www.mises.org/library/lemons-and-nobel-prize.

Ariew, R. (1976), *Ockham's Razor: A Historical and Philosophical Analysis of Ockham's Principle of Parsimony*, Champaign-Urbana, IL: University of Illinois Press.

Armstrong, M. (1999), 'Optimal regulation with unknown demand and cost functions', *Journal of Economic Theory*, **84** (2), 196–215.

Arrow, K.J. and F. Hahn (1971), *General Competitive Analysis*, San Francisco, CA: Holden-Day.

Barthel, S. (1992), *Die Fiaker von Wien*, Vienna: Dachs-Verlagsgesellschaft.

Benkler, Y. (2004), 'Sharing nicely: on shareable goods and the emergence of sharing as a modality of economic production', *Yale Law Journal*, **114** (2), 120–34.

Bernhardt, A. (2014), 'Labor standards and the reorganization of work: gaps in data and research', IRLE Working Paper No. 100-14.

Bessant, J, R. Watts, T. Dalton and P. Smyth (2006), *Talking Policy: How Social Policy is Made*, Sydney: Allen & Unwin.

Blanchard, O. (2008), 'Neoclassical synthesis', in S.N. Durlauf and L.E. Blume (eds), *The New Palgrave Dictionary of Economics*, New York: Palgrave Macmillan, pp. 504–10.

Boettke, P. (ed.) (1994), *The Elgar Companion to Austrian Economics*, Aldershot, UK and Brookfield, VT, USA: Edward Elgar Publishing.

Boettke, P. (2008), 'Austrian School of Economics', in D. Henderson (ed.), *The Concise Encyclopedia of Economics*, accessed 29 May 016 at http://www.econlib.org/library/Enc/AustrianSchoolofEconomics.html.

Botsman, R. (2015), 'Defining the sharing economy: what is collaborative consumption – and what isn't?', accessed 20 May 2016 at http://www.fastcoexist.com/3046119/defining-the-sharing-economy-what-is-collaborative-consumption-and-what-isnt.

Botsman, R. and R. Rogers (2010), *What's Mine is Yours. The Rise of Collaborative Consumption*, New York: HarperBusiness.

Bouchard, F. (2011), 'Darwinism without populations: a more inclusive understanding of the survival of the fittest', *Studies in History and Philosophy of Science, Part C: Studies in History and Philosophy of Biological and Biomedical Sciences*, **42** (1), 106–14.

Boyer, K.D. (1987), 'The costs of price regulation: lessons from railroad deregulation', *RAND Journal of Economics*, **18** (3), 408–16.

Brodbeck, K.H. (1991), 'Wirtschaft als autopoietisches System? Anmerkungen zu N. Luhmanns Buch Die Wirtschaft der Gesellschaft', *Zeitschrift für Politik*, **38** (3), 317–26.

Buchanan, J.M. (1959), 'Positive economics, welfare economics, and political economy', *Journal of Law and Economics*, **2** (2), 124–38.

Buckley, C. (2015), 'An examination of taxi apps and public policy regulation', accessed 29 May 2016 at http://www.clarebuckley.ca/pdf/Clare%20Buckley%20-%20public%20policy%20regulation.pdf.

Chase, R. (2015), *Peers Inc: How People and Platforms are Inventing the Collaborative Economy and Reinventing Capitalism*, New York: Public Affairs.

Christensen, C. (1995), 'Disruptive technologies catching the wave', *Harvard Business Review*, **73** (1), 3–5.

Christensen, C. (1997), *The Innovator's Dilemma*, Boston, MA: Harvard Business School Press.

Christensen, C. (2006), 'The ongoing process of building a theory of disruption', *Journal of Product Innovation Management*, **23** (1), 39–55.

Christensen, C., M. Johnson and H. Kagermann (2008), 'Reinventing your business model', *Harvard Business Review*, **86** (12), 57–68.

Christensen, C., J. Dyer and H. Gregersen (2013), *The Innovator's DNA: Mastering the Five Skills of Disruptive Innovators*, Boston, MA: Harvard Business School Press.

Christensen, C., M. Raynor and R. McDonald (2015), 'What is disruptive innovation?', *Harvard Business Review*, **93** (12), 44–53.

Cicala, S. (2014), 'When does regulation distort costs? Lessons from fuel procurement in U.S. electricity generation', National Bureau of Economic Research, Working Paper No. 20109.

Cochrane, J. (2014), 'Cost–benefit analysis as a framework for financial regulation', SSRN, accessed 29 May 2016 at ssrn.com/abstract=2425885.

Cohen, B. and J. Kietzmann (2014), 'Ride on! Mobility business models for the sharing economy', *Organization & Environment*, **27** (3), 279–96.

Cser, K. and A. Ohuchi (2008), 'World practices of hotel classification systems', *Asia Pacific Journal of Tourism Research*, **13** (4), 379–98.

Davidson, D. (1973), 'Radical interpretation', *Dialectica*, **27** (1), 314–28.

Davis, G.F. (2015), 'What might replace the modern corporation: Uberization and the web page enterprise', *Seattle University Law Review*, **39** (11), 501–14.

Dempsey, P. (1996), 'Taxi industry regulation, deregulation, and reregulation: the paradox of market failure', *Transportation Law Journal*, **24** (1), 73–120.

Diamond Jr, A. (2014), 'The creative destruction of labor policy', *Libertarian Papers*, **6**, 107–21.

Dickens, P. (2000), *Social Darwinism: Linking Evolutionary Thought to Social Theory*, Buckingham: Open University Press.

Diggins, J.P. (1978), *The Bard of Savagery: Thorstein Veblen and Modern Social Theory*, Hassocks, Sussex: Harvester Press.

Edelman, B. and D. Geradin (2015), 'Efficiencies and regulatory shortcuts: how should we regulate companies like Airbnb and Uber?', Harvard Business School NOM Unit, Working Paper No. 16-026.

Elliott, J. (1980), 'Marx and Schumpeter on capitalism's creative destruction: a comparative restatement', *Quarterly Journal of Economics*, **95** (1), 45–68.

Epstein, R. (2005), 'Monopoly dominance or level playing field? The new antitrust paradox', *University of Chicago Law Review*, **72** (1), 49–72.

Epstein, S.R. and M. Prak (eds) (2008), *Guilds, Innovation and the European Economy, 1400–1800*, Cambridge: Cambridge University Press.

Ferrell, O. and M. Hartline (2012), *Marketing Strategy, Text and Cases*, Cincinnati, OH: South-Western College Publications.

Flohr, A. (2014), *Self-regulation and Legalization: Making Global Rules for Banks and Corporations*, New York: Palgrave Macmillan.

Foxall, G. (2014), *Corporate Innovation: Marketing and Strategy*, London: Routledge.

Frazier, N. (2001), *William Randolph Hearst: Modern Media Tycoon*, Woodbridge, CT: Blackbirch Press.

Frieden, J. and P. Kennedy (2006), *Global Capitalism: Its Fall and Rise in the Twentieth Century*, New York: W.W. Norton.

Gapiński, A. (2016), 'Licensure, ethics, welfare of the public and Uberization of services', *Warsztaty menedżerskie*, **16** (1), 49–56.

Gilpin, R. and J. Gilpin (2000), *The Challenge of Global Capitalism: The World Economy in the 21st Century*, Princeton, NJ: Princeton University Press.

Grassl, W. and B. Smith (eds) (1986), *Austrian Economics. Historical and Philosophical Background*, New York: New York University Press.

Guo, Y. and J. Tang (2015), 'Barriers and legal solutions to e-logistics in China', in Y. Guo (ed.), *Research on Selected China's Legal Issues of E-business*, Berlin: Springer, pp. 73–87.

Hall, J. and A. Kruger (2015), 'An analysis of the labor market for Uber's driver-partners in the United States', accessed 29 May 2016 at irs.princeton.edu/sites/irs/files/An%20Analysis%20of%20the%20Labor %20Market%20for%20Uber%E2%80%99s%20Driver-Partners%20in %20the%20United%20States%20587.pdf.

Hamari, J., M. Sjöklint and A. Ukkonen (2015), 'The sharing economy: why people participate in collaborative consumption', *Journal of the Association for Information Science and Technology*, **15** (1), DOI: 10.1002/asi.23552.

Hansmann, H. and R. Kraakman (2000), 'The end of history for corporate law', Harvard Law School John M. Olin Center for Law, Economics and Business Discussion Paper Series No. 3-7-2000.

Harris, P. (2010), *The Architectural Achievement of Joseph Aloysius Hansom (1803–1882), Designer of the Hansom Cab, Birmingham Town Hall, and Churches of the Catholic Revival*, London: The Edwin Mellen Press.

Hart, H. (1961), *The Concept of Law*, Oxford: Oxford University Press.

Hodges, G. (2009), *Taxi!: A Social History of the New York City Cabdriver*, New York: New York University Press.

Hodgson, G. (1997), 'The evolutionary and non-Darwinian economics of Joseph Schumpeter', *Journal of Evolutionary Economics*, **7** (2), 131–45.

Hovenga, C., D. Naik and W. Block (2013), 'The detrimental side effects of minimum wage laws', *Business and Society Review*, **118** (4), 463–87.

Johnson, G., K. Scholes and R. Whittington (2008), *Exploring Corporate Strategy: Text and Cases*, New York: Pearson Education.

Katz, E. (1988), 'Disintermediation: cutting out the middle man', *Intermedia*, **16** (2), 30–38.

Keele, R. (2010), *Ockham Explained: From Razor to Rebellion*, Chicago and La Salle, IL: Open Court.

Kelm, M. (1997), 'Schumpeter's theory of economic evolution: a Darwinian interpretation', *Journal of Evolutionary Economics*, **7** (2), 97–130.

Kirzner, I. (1976), 'Equilibrium versus market process', in E. Dolan (ed.), *The Foundations of Modern Austrian Economics*, accessed 29 May 2016 at http://www.econlib.org/library/NPDBooks/Dolan/dlnFMA7.html.

Kirzner, I. (1996), *The Meaning of Market Process. Essays in the Development of Modern Austrian Economics*, London: Routledge.

Knoll, M. (2007), 'The UBIT: leveling an uneven playing field or tilting a level one?', *Fordham Law Review*, **76** (3), 857–69.

Laffey, D. (2006), 'The rise and fall of the dot com enterprises', in A. Burke (ed.), *Modern Perspectives on Entrepreneurship*, Dublin: Senate Hall Academic Publishing, pp. 111–45.

Lepore, J. (2014), 'The disruption machine: what the gospel of innovation gets wrong', *The New Yorker*, 23 June, accessed 29 May 2016 at http://www.newyorker.com/reporting/2014/06/23/140623fa_fact_lepore?currentPage=all.

Listl, G. and W. Dammann (2009), 'Untersuchungen zum Einsatz von Taxi-Floating Car Data im Ballungsraum Rhein-Main' ('Studies for the application of taxi floating car data in the Rhine-Main-area'), *Strassenverkehrstechnik*, **53** (3), 114–31.

Martenet, V. and A. Heinemann (2012), *Droit de la concurrence*, Geneva: Quid iuris.

McBride, S. (2015), 'Ridesourcing and the taxi marketplace', Dissertation thesis submitted to Boston College, College of Arts and Sciences.

McCraw, T. (2006), 'Schumpeter's business cycles as business history', *Business History Review*, **80** (2), 231–61.

Mises, Ludwig von (1927), *Liberalismus*, Jena: Verlag von Gustav Fischer.

Mises, Ludwig von (1933), *Epistemological Problems of Economics*, English language edition 1960, Auburn, AL: Ludwig von Mises Institute.

Mises, Ludwig von (1949), *Human Action: A Treatise on Economics*, New Haven, CT: Yale University Press.

Möhlmann, M. (2015), 'Collaborative consumption: determinants of satisfaction and the likelihood of using a sharing economy option again', *Journal of Consumer Behaviour*, **14** (3), 193–207.

Morse, H.B. (1909), *The Guilds of China*, London: Longmans, Green & Co.

Motta, M. (2004), *Competition Policy. Theory and Practice*, Cambridge: Cambridge University Press.

Müller, A. (1983), *Die Marxsche Konjunkturtheorie – Eine überakkumulationstheoretische Interpretation*, Cologne: PapyRossa.

Neef, A. (2008), *Kartellrecht*, Heidelberg: C.F. Müller Verlag.

Nunes, B., D. Bennett and D. Shaw (2013), '8 steps for managing green innovation in the automotive industry', *European Financial Review*, **13** (June–July), 3–6.

OECD (2014), *The Governance of Regulators, OECD Best Practice Principles for Regulatory Policy*, Paris: OECD Publishing.

Paul, D. (1988), 'The selection of the survival of the fittest', *Journal of the History of Biology*, **21** (3), 411–24.

Perry, M. (2015), 'Creative destruction: top 20 reasons ride-sharing is better than taxis and represents the future of transportation', accessed 29 May 2016 at http://www.aei.org/publication/creative-destruction-top-20-reasons-ride-sharing-is-better-than-taxis-and-represents-the-future-of-transportation/.

Posner, R. (2009), *Antitrust Law*, Chicago, IL: University of Chicago Press.

Rauch, D. and D. Schleicher (2015), 'Like Uber, but for local governmental policy: the future of local regulation of the sharing economy', George Mason Law & Economics Research Paper No. 15-01.

Reetz, N. (2005), *Grundlagen der mikroökonomischen Theorie*, St Gallen: Surbir.

Rogers, B. (2015), 'The social costs of Uber', *University of Chicago Law Review Dialogue*, **82** (3), 85–103.

Rosemont Jr, H. (2015), *Against Individualism: A Confucian Rethinking of the Foundations of Morality, Politics, Family, and Religion*, New York: Rowman & Littlefield.

Ross, D. (2014), *Philosophy of Economics*, London: Palgrave Macmillan.

Rugman, A. and S. Girod (2003), 'Retail multinationals and globalization: the evidence is regional', *European Management Journal*, **21** (1), 24–37.

Salnikov, V., R. Lambiotte, A. Noulas and C. Mascolo (2015), 'OpenStreetCab: exploiting taxi mobility patterns in New York City to reduce commuter costs', accessed 29 May 2016 at arxiv.org/pdf/1503.03021v1.pdf.

Schmitt, V. and C. Sommer (2013), 'Mobilfalt – ein Mitnahmesystem als Ergänzung des ÖPNV in ländlichen Räumen', in H. Proff, W. Pascha, J. Schönharting and D. Schramm (eds), *Schritte in die künftige Mobilität*, Wiesbaden: Springer, pp. 401–13.

Schneider, H. (2013), 'Wettbewerb der Wettbewerbsbehörden?', *sic!*, **13** (11), 690–98.

Schneider, H. (2014), 'The market: a philosophic approach', Lecture series delivered in Kosovo and France (partially published in *Eigentümlich frei* 2015).

Schneider, H. (2015), 'The Uber effect', *Eigentümlich frei*, **15** (8), 61–2.

Schor, J. (2014), 'Debating the sharing economy', Great Transition Initiative, accessed 29 May 2016 at http://www.geo.coop/sites/default/files/schor_debating_the_sharing_economy.pdf.

Schulak, E.-M. and H. Unterköfler (2011), *The Austrian School of Economics: A History of its Ideas, Ambassadors, and Institutions*, Auburn, AL: Ludwig von Mises Institute.

Schumpeter, J.A. (1911), *Theorie der wirtschaftlichen Entwicklung: eine Untersuchung über Unternehmergewinn, Kapital, Kredit, Zins und den Konjunkturzyklus*, Hamburg: Dunker.

Schumpeter, J.A. (1939), *Business Cycles: A Theoretical, Historical, and Statistical Analysis of the Capitalist Process*, New York, Toronto and London: McGraw-Hill Book Company.

Schumpeter, J.A. (1942), *Capitalism, Socialism, and Democracy*, New York: Harper and Brothers.

Searle, J. (1995), *The Construction of Social Reality*, New York: Simon and Schuster.

Seldon, A. (2004), *The Virtues of Capitalism*, New York: Liberty Fund.

Smith, P. (1998), *Explaining Chaos*, Cambridge: Cambridge University Press.

Stalder, F. (2011), 'Ethics of sharing', *Ethics*, **15** (1), 9–21.

Summers, L. and E. Balls (eds) (2015), *Report of the Commission for Inclusive Prosperity*, Washington, DC: Center for American Progress.

Sunder, S. (2002), 'Regulatory competition among accounting standards within and across international boundaries', *Journal of Accounting and Public Policy*, **21** (3), 219–34.

Time Magazine (2014), 'A historical argument against Uber: taxi regulations are there for a reason', 19 November, accessed 29 May 2016 at time.com/3592035/uber-taxi-history/.

Ulrich, P. (2008), *Integrative Economic Ethics: Foundations of a Civilized Market Economy*, Cambridge: Cambridge University Press.

Veltrop, D. and J. de Haan (2014), 'I just cannot get you out of my head: regulatory capture of financial sector supervisors', De Nederlandsche Bank Working Paper No. 410.

Williamson, O. (1979), 'Transaction-cost economics: the governance of contractual relations', *Journal of Law and Economics*, **22** (2), 233–61.

Winker, P. (1996), *Rationierung auf dem Markt für Unternehmenskredite in der BRD*, Tübimgen: Mohr Siebeck.

Wired (2014), 'Uber's biggest danger is its business model, not bad PR', accessed 29 May 2016 at http://www.wired.com/2014/08/the-peril-to-uber-is-its-business-model-not-bad-pr/.

Wittgenstein, L. (1945), *Philosophische Untersuchungen* [*Philosophical Investigations*], Frankfurt: Suhrkamp.

Wu, H. and J. Yong (2013), 'Assessment of service quality in the hotel industry', *Journal of Quality Assurance in Hospitality & Tourism*, **14** (3), 218–44.

Wyman, K. (2013), 'Problematic private property: the case of New York taxicab medallions', *Yale Journal on Regulation*, **30** (2), 125–42.

Yang, H., S. Wong, S. Chung and K. Wong (2002), 'Demand–supply equilibrium of taxi services in a network under competition and regulation', *Transportation Research*, **36** (9), 799–819.

Zäch, R. (2005), *Schweizerisches Kartellrecht*, Bern: Stämpfli.

Index